THE MEANING OF
MASONRY

THE MEANING OF
MASONRY

W.L. WILMSHURST
P.M. 275; PAST PROVINCIAL
GRAND REGISTRAR
(WEST YORKS.)

GRAMERCY BOOKS
New York

This volume contains the complete unabridged texts of the original editions.
They have been complete reset for this volume.

This edition is published by Gramercy Books,
an imprint of Random House Value Publishing,
a division of Random House, Inc., New York.

Gramercy is a registered trademark and the colophon is a trademark
of Random House, Inc.

Random House
New York • Toronto • London • Sydney • Auckland
www.randomhouse.com

Printed and bound in the United States of America

Library of Congress Cataloging-in-Publication Data

Wilmhurst, Walter Leslie, 1867–
The meaning of Masonry

Reprint of the 5th ed. (1927) published by Rider, London.
1.Freemasons—symbolism. I. Title.
I. Title. II. Title: Selected works.
HS425.W56   1980   336'.1   80-23196

ISBN 0-517-33194-2

25 24 23 22 21 20 19 18 17 16

CONTENTS

FOREWORD   3

INTRODUCTION
The Position and Possibilities of the
    Masonic Order   5

CHAPTER I
The Deeper Symbolism of Masonry   19

CHAPTER II
Masonry as a Philosophy   54

CHAPTER III
Further Notes on Craft Symbolism   87

CHAPTER IV
The Holy Royal Arch   138

CHAPTER V
The Relation of Masonry to the Ancient
    Mysteries   170

'WE must, then, demonstrate that ours is a Hierarchy of inspired, divine and deifying science, of efficacy and of consecration for those initiated with the initiation of the revelation derived from the hierarchical mysteries.

Head of this Hierarchy is the Fountain of Life, the Essence of Goodness, the one Triad, Cause of things that be,......assimilation to and union with Whom, as far as attainable, is deification.

And this is the common goal of every Hierarchy, —persistent devotion towards God and divine things divinely and uniformly ministered; prior to which there must be a complete and unswerving removal of things contrary; a knowledge of things as they are in themselves; the vision and science of sacred truth; the inspired communication of the uniform perfection of the One Itself, as far as attainable; the banquet of contemplation, nourishing intelligibly and deifying every man elevated towards it."

DIONYSIUS AREOPAGITICUS,
De Eccles. Hierarch., 1, 1-3.

Foreword

FREEMASONRY has had many great scholars who devoted their time and talents to the philosophical exposition of the character of the Craft, the meaning of Craft symbols, and the religious aspects of the Fraternity: Albert Pike, Robert Freke Gould, Fort Newton, Albert Gallatin Mackey, and W. L. Wilmshurst.

Walter Leslie Wilmshurst (1867–1939) was a mystic with a practical knowledge and profound understanding of the religions of the world. *The Meaning of Masonry* discloses the real purpose of modern Freemasonry and clearly states the true body of teaching and practice concerning the esoteric meanings of Masonic ritual.

Freemasonry is based on the three great principles: brotherly love, relief, and truth. Over the years, brotherly love and relief have been so stressed that the Craft is in serious danger of becoming primarily a social and charitable organization. Truth, the most difficult principle to recognize and thus the most difficult to achieve, has long been neglected. Wilmshurst carefully places his designs upon the trestle board to build his thesis that the alpha and omega of Freemasonry is not the repetition of the ritual nor the safeguarding of secrets, but the regeneration of the Brethren.

This book implores the reader to learn to see in Freemasonry something more than a parochial system enjoining elementary morality, performing perfunctory and insignificant rites, and serving as an agreeable accessory to social life. The greater system of spiritual doctrine contained in the rituals is strongly emphasized.

The Meaning of Masonry was written with a view toward promoting a deeper understanding of the Fraternity, and this goal has been achieved. The ideals of the Masonic Fraternity have a wide appeal to the best instincts of men, and the Craft has become one of the greatest social institutions in the world. In this new Aquarian age, when many individuals and groups are working in various ways for the eventual restoration of the mysteries, an increasing number of aspirants are beginning to recognize that Freemasonry may well be the vehicle for this achievement.

We have here a sincere effort by a learned and earnest Brother to point to the source of Masonic Light in elegant, and at times profound, language. They who look with him may enjoy the same felicity.

The great value of this book is that it was written by one who sets an example for all Masters of Lodges. His was a soul filled with the wonder of wisdom, strength, and beauty. In these pages, he whispers the password to those of us who still clamor at the gate, enabling us to enter that inner chamber where we can join the true initiates and share experiences now veiled from all but a handful of Brethren.

ALLAN BOUDREAU, PH.D.
Curator and Librarian
Grand Lodge of Free and Accepted
July, 1980   Masons of the State of New York

Introduction
THE POSITION AND POSSIBILITIES OF THE MASONIC ORDER

THE papers here collected are written solely for members of the Masonic Order, constituted under the United Grand Lodge of England. To all such they are offered in the best spirit of fraternity and goodwill and with the wish to render to the Order some small return for the profit the author has received from his association with it extending over thirty-two years. They have been written with a view to promoting the deeper understanding of the meaning of Masonry; to providing the explanation of it that one constantly hears called for and that becomes all the more necessary in view of the unprecedented increase of interest in, and membership of, the Order at the present day.

The meaning of Masonry, however, is a subject usually left entirely unexpounded and that accordingly remains largely unrealized by its members save such few as make it their private study; the authorities of what in all other respects is an elaborately organized and admirably controlled community have hitherto made no provision for explaining and teaching the " noble science " which Masonry proclaims itself to be and was certainly designed to impart. It seems taken for granted that reception into the Order will automatically be accompanied by an ability to appreciate forthwith and at its full value all that one there finds. The contrary is the case, for Masonry is a veiled and

The Meaning of Masonry cryptic expression of the difficult science of spiritual life, and the understanding of it calls for special and informed guidance on the one hand, and on the other a genuine and earnest desire for knowledge and no small capacity for spiritual perception on the part of those seeking to be instructed ; and not infrequently one finds Brethren discontinuing their interest or their membership because they find that Masonry means nothing to them and that no explanation or guidance is vouchsafed them. Were such instruction provided, assimilated and responded to, the life of the Order would be enormously quickened and deepened and its efficiency as a means of Initiation intensified, whilst incidentally the fact would prove an added safeguard against the admission into the Order of unsuitable members—by which is meant not merely persons who fail to satisfy conventional qualifications, but also those who, whilst fitted in these respects, are as yet either so intellectually or spiritually unprogressed as to be incapable of benefiting from Initiation in its true sense although passing formally through Initiation rites. Spiritual quality rather than numbers, ability to understand the Masonic system and reduce its implications into personal experience rather than the perfunctory conferment of its rites, are the desiderata of the Craft to-day.

As a contribution to repairing the absence of explanation referred to these papers have been compiled. The first two of them have often been read as lectures at Lodge meetings. Many requests that they should be printed and made more widely available led to my expanding their subject-matter into greater detail than could be used for occasional lectures, and accordingly they are here amplified by a paper containing fuller notes upon Craft symbolism. To complete the consideration of the Craft system it was necessary also to add a chapter upon that which forms the crown and culmination of the Craft Degrees and without which they would be imperfect—the Order of the Royal Arch. Lastly a chapter has been added upon the important subject which forms the background of the rest—the relationship of modern Masonry to the Ancient Mysteries, from which it is the direct, though greatly attenuated, spiritual descendant.

Thus in the five papers I have sought to provide a survey of the whole Masonic subject as expressed by the Craft and Arch Degrees, which it is hoped may prove illuminating to the increasing number of Brethren who feel that Freemasonry enshrines something deeper and greater than, in the absence of guidance, they have been able to realize. It does not profess to be more than an elementary and far from exhaustive survey; the subject might be treated much more fully, in more technical terminology and with abundant references to authorities, were one compiling a more ambitious and scholarly treatise. But to the average Mason such a treatise would probably prove less serviceable than a summary expressed in as simple and untechnical terms as may be and unburdened by numerous literary references. Some repetition, due to the papers having been written at different times, may be found in later chapters of points already dealt with in previous ones, though the restatement may be advantageous in emphasizing those points and maintaining continuity of exposition. For reasons explained in the chapter itself, that on the Holy Royal Arch will probably prove difficult of comprehension by those unversed in the literature and psychology of religious mysticism ; if so, the reading of it may be deferred or neglected. But since a survey of the Masonic system would, like the system itself, be incomplete without reference to that supreme Degree, and since that Degree deals with matters of advanced psychological and spiritual experience about which explanation must always be difficult, the subject has been treated here with as much simplicity of statement as is possible and rather with a view to indicating to what great heights of spiritual attainment the Craft Degrees point as achievable, than with the expectation that they will be readily comprehended by readers without some measure of mystical experience and perhaps unfamiliar with the testimony of the mystics thereto.

Purposely these papers avoid dealing with matters of Craft history and of merely antiquarian or archæological interest. Dates, particulars of Masonic constitutions, historical changes and developments in the external aspects of the Craft, references to old Lodges and the names of outstanding people connected therewith—these and such like matters can be read about elsewhere. They are all subordinate to what alone is of vital moment and what so many Brethren are hungering for—knowledge of the spiritual purpose and lineage of the Order and the present-day value of rites of Initiation.

In giving these pages to publication care has been

8

taken to observe due reticence in respect of essential matters. The general nature of the Masonic system is, however, nowadays widely known to outsiders and easily ascertainable from many printed sources, whilst the large interest in and output of literature upon mystical religion and the science of the inward life during the last few years has familiarized many with a subject of which, as is shown in these papers, Masonry is but a specialized form. To explain Masonry in general outline is, therefore, not to divulge a subject which is entirely exclusive to its members, but merely to show that Masonry stands in line with other doctrinal systems inculcating the same principles and to which no secrecy attaches, and that it is a specialized and highly effective method of inculcating those principles. Truth, whether as expressed in Masonry or otherwise, is at all times an open secret, but is as a pillar of light to those able to receive and profit by it, and to all others but one of darkness and unintelligibility. An elementary and formal secrecy is requisite as a practical precaution against the intrusion of improper persons and for preventing profanation. In other respects the vital secrets of life, and of any system expounding life, protect themselves even though shouted from the housetops, because they mean nothing to those as yet unqualified for the knowledge and unready to identify themselves with it by incorporating it into their habitual thought and conduct.

In view of the great spread and popularity of Masonry to-day—when there are some three

thousand Lodges in Great Britain alone—it is as
well to consider its present bearings and tendencies
and to give a thought to future possibilities. The
Order is a semi-secret, semi-public institution ;
secret in respect of its activities *intra mœnia*, but
otherwise of full public notoriety, with its doors
open to any applicant for admission who is of
ordinary good character and repute. Those who
enter it, as the majority do, entirely ignorant of what
they will find there, usually because they have friends
there or know Masonry to be an institution devoted
to high ideals and benevolence and with which it
may be socially desirable to be connected, may or
may not be attracted and profit by what is disclosed
to them, and may or may not see anything beyond
the bare form of the symbol or hear anything beyond
the mere letter of the word. Their admission is
quite a lottery ; their Initiation too often remains
but a formality, not an actual awakening into an
order and quality of life previously unexperienced ;
their membership, unless such an awakening eventually ensues from the careful study and faithful
practice of the Order's teaching, has little, if any,
greater influence upon them than would ensue from
their joining a purely social club.

For " Initiation "—for which there are so many
candidates little conscious of what is implied in that
for which they ask—what does it really mean and
intend ? It means a new beginning (*initium*) ; a
break-away from an old method and order of life
and the entrance upon a new one of larger self-
knowledge, deepened understanding and intensified
virtue. It means a transition from the merely

10

natural state and standards of life towards a regenerate and super-natural state and standard. It means a turning away from the pursuit of the popular ideals of the outer world, in the conviction that those ideals are but shadows, images and temporal substitutions for the eternal Reality that underlies them, to the keen and undivertible quest of that Reality itself and the recovery of those genuine secrets of our being which lie buried and hidden at " the centre " or innermost part of our souls. It means the awakening of those hitherto dormant higher faculties of the soul which endue their possessor with " light " in the form of new enhanced consciousness and enlarged perceptive faculty. And lastly, in words with which every Mason is familiar, it means that the postulant will henceforth dedicate and devote his life to the Divine rather than to his own or any other service, so that by the principles of the Order he may be the better enabled to display that beauty of godliness which previously perhaps has not manifested through him.

To comply with this definition of Initiation— which it might be useful to apply as a test not only to those who seek for admission into the Order, but to ourselves who are already within it—it is obvious that special qualifications of mind and intention are essential in a candidate of the type likely to be benefited by the Order in the way that its doctrine contemplates, and that it is not necessarily the ordinary man of the world, personal friend and good fellow though he be according to usual social standards, who is either properly prepared for, or likely to benefit in any vital sense by, reception into

it. The true candidate must indeed needs be, as
the word *candidus* implies, a " white man," white
within as symbolically he is white-vestured without,
so that no inward stain or soilure may obstruct the
dawn within his soul of that Light which he professes
to be the predominant wish of his heart on asking for
admission; whilst, if really desirous of learning the
secrets and mysteries of his own being, he must be
prepared to divest himself of all past preconceptions
and thought-habits and, with childlike meekness
and docility, surrender his mind to the reception
of some perhaps novel and unexpected truths
which Initiation promises to impart and which will
more and more unfold and justify themselves
within those, and those only, who are, and continue
to keep themselves, properly prepared for them.
" Know thyself ! " was the injunction inscribed over
the portals of ancient temples of Initiation, for with
that knowledge was promised the knowledge of all
secrets and all mysteries. And Masonry was
designed to teach self-knowledge. But self-
knowledge involves a knowledge much deeper,
vaster and more difficult than is popularly conceived.
It is not to be acquired by the formal passage through
three or four degrees in as many months; it is a
knowledge impossible of full achievement until
knowledge of every other kind has been laid aside
and a difficult path of life long and strenuously
pursued that alone fits and leads its followers to its
attainment. The wisest and most advanced of us
is perhaps still but an Entered Apprentice at this
knowledge, however high his titular rank. Here
and there may be one worthy of being hailed as a

Fellow-Craft in the true sense. The full Master-Mason—the just man made perfect who has actually and not merely ceremonially travelled the entire path, endured all its tests and ordeals, and become raised into conscious union with the Author and Giver of Life and able to mediate and impart that life to others—is at all times hard to find.

So high, so ideal an attainment, it may be urged, is beyond our reach; we are but ordinary men of the world sufficiently occupied already with our primary civic, social and family obligations and following the obvious normal path of natural life! Granted. Nevertheless to point to that attainment as possible to us and as our destiny, to indicate that path of self-perfecting to those who care and dare to follow it, modern Speculative Masonry was instituted, and to emphasizing the fact these papers are devoted. For Masonry means this or it means nothing worth the serious pursuit of thoughtful men; nothing that cannot be pursued as well outside the Craft as within it. It proclaims the fact that there exists a higher and more secret path of life than that which we normally tread, and that when the outer world and its pursuits and rewards lose their attractiveness for us and prove insufficient to our deeper needs, as sooner or later they will, we are compelled to turn back upon ourselves, to seek and knock at the door of a world within; and it is upon this inner world, and the path to and through it, that Masonry promises light, charts the way, and indicates the qualifications and conditions of progress. This is the sole aim and intention of Masonry. Behind its more elementary and obvious

13

symbolism, behind its counsels to virtue and conventional morality, behind the platitudes and sententious phraseology (which nowadays might well be subjected to competent and intelligent revision) with which, after the fashion of their day, the eighteenth-century compilers of its ceremonies clothed its teaching, there exists the framework of a scheme of initiation into that higher path of life where alone the secrets and mysteries of our being are to be learned ; a scheme moreover that, as will be shown later in these pages, reproduces for the modern world the main features of the Ancient Mysteries, and that has been well described by a learned writer on the subject as " an epitome or reflection at a far distance of the once universal science."

But because, for long and for many, Masonry has meant less than this, it has not as yet fulfilled its original purpose of being the efficient initiating instrument it was designed to be ; its energies have been diverted from its true instructional purpose into social and philanthropic channels, excellent in their way, but foreign to and accretions upon the primal main intention. Indeed, so little perceived or appreciated is that central intention that one frequently hears it confessed by men of eminent position in the Craft and warm devotion to it that only their interest in its great charitable institutions keeps alive their connection with the Order. Relief is indeed a duty incumbent upon a Mason, but its Masonic interpretation is not meant to be limited to physical necessities. The spiritually as well as the financially poor and distressed are always with

14

us and to the former, equally with the latter, Masonry was designed to minister. Theoretically every man upon reception into the Craft acknowledges himself as within the category of the spiritually poor, and as content to renounce all temporal riches if haply by that sacrifice his hungry heart may be filled with those good things which money cannot purchase, but to which the truly initiated can help him.

But if Masonry has not as yet fulfilled its primary purpose and, though engaged in admirable secondary activities, is as yet an initiating instrument of low efficiency, it may be that, with enlarged understanding of its designs, that efficiency may yet become very considerably increased. During the last two centuries the Craft has been gradually developing from small and crude beginnings into its present vast and highly elaborated organization. To-day the number of Lodges and the membership of the Craft are increasing beyond all precedent. One asks oneself what this growing interest portends, and to what it will, or can be made to, lead? The growth synchronizes with a corresponding defection of interest in orthodox religion and public worship. It need not now be enquired whether or to what extent the simple principles of faith and the humanitarian ideals of Masonry are with some men taking the place of the theology offered in the various Churches; it is probable that to some extent they do so. But the fact is with us that the ideals of the Masonic Order are making a wide appeal to the best instincts of large numbers of men and that the Order has imperceptibly become the greatest social institution in the Empire. Its principles of faith and

15

ethics are simple, and of virtually universal
acceptance. Providing means for the expression of
universal fraternity under a common Divine Father-
hood and of a common loyalty to the headship and
established government of the State, it leaves room
for divergences of private belief and view upon
matters upon which unity is impracticable and
perhaps undesirable. It is utterly clean of politics
and political intrigue, but nevertheless has unconsciously become a real, though unobtrusive, asset of
political value, both in stabilizing the social fabric
and tending to foster international amity. The
elaborateness of its organization, the care and
admirable control of its affairs by its higher
authorities, are praiseworthy in the extreme, whilst
in the conduct of its individual Lodges there has
been and is a progressive endeavour to raise the
standard of ceremonial work to a far higher degree
of reverence and intelligence than was perhaps
possible under conditions existing not long ago.
The Masonic Craft has grown and ramified to
dimensions undreamed of by its original founders
and, at its present rate of increase, its potentialities
and influence in the future are quite incalculable.

What seems now needed to intensify the worth
and usefulness of this great Brotherhood is to deepen
its understanding of its own system, to educate its
members in the deeper meaning and true purpose
of its rites and its philosophy. Were this achieved
the Masonic Order would become, in proportion to
that achievement, a spiritual force greater than it
can ever be so long as it continues content with a
formal and unintelligent perpetuation of rites, the

real and sacred purpose of which remains largely unperceived, and participation in which too often means nothing more than association with an agreeable, semi-religious, social institution. Carried to its fullest, that achievement would involve the revival, in a form adapted to modern conditions, of the ancient Wisdom-teaching and the practice of those Mysteries which became proscribed fifteen centuries ago, but of which modern Masonry is the direct and representative descendant, as will appear later in these pages.

The future development and the value of the Order as a moral force in society depend, therefore, upon the view its members take of their system. If they do not spiritualize it they will but increasingly materialize it. If they fail to interpret its veiled purport, to enter into the understanding of its underlying philosophy, and to translate its symbolism into what is signified thereby, they will be mistaking shadow for substance, a husk for the kernel, and secularizing what was designed as a means of spiritual instruction and grace. It is from lack of instruction rather than of desire to learn the meaning of Masonry that the Craft suffers to-day. But, as one finds everywhere, that desire exists ; and so, for what they may be worth, these papers are offered to the Craft as a contribution towards satisfying it.

Let me conclude with an apologue and an aspiration.

In the *Chronicles* of Israel it may be read how that, after long preparatory labour, after employing the choicest material and the most skilful artificers,

Solomon the King at last made an end of building
and beautifying his Temple, and dedicated to the
service of the Most High that work of his hands in
a state as perfect as human provision could make it;
and how that then, but not till then, his offering was
accepted and the acceptance was signified by a
Divine descent upon it so that the glory of the Lord
shone through and filled the whole house.

So—if we will have it so—may it be with the
temple of the Masonic Order. Since the inception
of Speculative Masonry it has been a-building and
expanding now these last three hundred years.
Fashioned of living stones into a far-reaching organic
structure; brought gradually, under the good
guidance of its rulers, to high perfection on its
temporal side and in respect of its external obser-
vances, and made available for high purposes and
giving godly witness in a dark and troubled world;
upon these preliminary efforts let there now be
invoked this crowning and completing blessing—
that the Spirit of Wisdom and Understanding may
descend upon the work of our hands in abundant
measure, prospering it still farther, and filling and
transfiguring our whole Masonic house.

Chapter I.

THE DEEPER SYMBOLISM OF FREEMASONRY

A CANDIDATE proposing to enter Freemasonry has seldom formed any definite idea of the nature of what he is engaging in. Even after his admission he usually remains quite at a loss to explain satisfactorily what Masonry is and for what purpose his Order exists. He finds, indeed, that it is " a system of morality veiled in allegory and illustrated by symbols," but that explanation, whilst true, is but partial and does not carry him very far. For many members of the Craft to be a Mason implies merely connection with a body which seems to be something combining the natures of a club and a benefit society. They find, of course, a certain religious element in it, but as they are told that religious discussion, which means, of course, sectarian religious discussion, is forbidden in the Lodge, they infer that Masonry is not a religious institution, and that its teachings are intended to be merely secondary and supplemental to any religious tenets they may happen to hold. One sometimes hears it remarked that Masonry is " not a religion " ; which in a sense is quite true ; and sometimes that it is a secondary or supplementary religion, which is quite untrue. Again Masonry is often supposed, even by its own members, to be a system of extreme antiquity, that was practised and that has come down in well-nigh its present form from Egyptian or at least from early Hebrew sources :

19

a view which again possesses the merest modicum of truth. In brief, the vaguest notions obtain about the origin and history of the Craft, whilst the still more vital subject of its immediate and present purpose, and of its possibilities, remains almost entirely outside the consciousness of many of its own members. We meet in our Lodges regularly; we perform our ceremonial work and repeat our catechetical instruction-lectures night after night with a less or greater degree of intelligence and verbal perfection, and there our work ends, as though the ability to perform this work creditably were the be-all and the end-all of Masonic work. Seldom or never do we employ our Lodge meetings for that purpose for which, quite as much as for ceremonial purposes, they were intended, *viz. :* for " expatiating on the mysteries of the Craft," and perhaps our neglect to do so is because we have ourselves imperfectly realized what those mysteries are into which our Order was primarily formed to introduce us.

Yet, there exists a large number of brethren who would willingly repair this obvious deficiency; brethren to whose natures Masonry, even in their more limited aspect of it, makes a profound appeal, and who feel their membership of the Craft to be a privilege which has brought them into the presence of something greater than they know, and that enshrines a purpose and that could unfold a message deeper than they at present realize.

In a brief address like this it is hopeless to attempt to deal at all adequately with what I have suggested are deficiencies in our knowledge of the system we

20

belong to. The most one can hope to do is to offer a few hints or clues, which those who so desire may develop for themselves in the privacy of their own thought. For in the last resource no one *can* communicate the deeper things in Masonry to another. Every man must discover and learn them for himself, although a friend or brother may be able to conduct him a certain distance on the path of understanding. We know that even the elementary and superficial secrets of the Order must not be communicated to unqualified persons, and the reason for this injunction is not so much because those secrets have any special value, but because that silence is intended to be typical of that which applies to the greater, deeper secrets, some of which, for appropriate reasons, must not be communicated, and some of which indeed are not communicable at all, because they transcend the power of communication.

It is well to emphasize then, at the outset, that Masonry is a sacramental system, possessing, like all sacraments, an outward and visible side consisting of its ceremonial, its doctrine and its symbols which we can see and hear, and an inward, intellectual and spiritual side, which is concealed behind the ceremonial, the doctrine and the symbols, and which is available only to the Mason who has learned to use his spiritual imagination and who can appreciate the reality that lies behind the veil of outward symbol. Anyone, of course, can understand the simpler meaning of our symbols, especially with the help of the explanatory lectures ; but he may still miss the meaning of the scheme as a vital whole. It is absurd to think that a vast organization like

Masonry was ordained merely to teach to grown-up men of the world the symbolical meaning of a few simple builders' tools, or to impress upon us such elementary virtues as temperance and justice :—the children in every village school are taught such things ; or to enforce such simple principles of morals as brotherly love, which every church and every religion teaches ; or as relief, which is practised quite as much by non-Masons as by us ; or of truth, which every infant learns upon its mother's knee. There is surely, too, no need for us to join a secret society to be taught that the volume of the Sacred Law is a fountain of truth and instruction ; or to go through the great and elaborate ceremony of the third degree merely to learn that we have each to die. The Craft whose work we are taught to honour with the name of a " science," a " royal art," has surely some larger end in view than merely inculcating the practice of social virtues common to all the world and by no means the monopoly of Freemasons. Surely, then, it behoves us to acquaint ourselves with what that larger end consists, to enquire why the fulfilment of that purpose is worthy to be called a science, and to ascertain what *are* those " mysteries " to which our doctrine promises we may ultimately attain if we apply ourselves assiduously enough to understanding what Masonry is capable of teaching us.

Realizing, then, what Masonry cannot be deemed to be, let us ask what it is. But before answering that question, let me put you in possession of certain facts that will enable you the better to appreciate the answer when I formulate it. In all periods of the world's history, and in every part of the globe, secret orders and societies have existed outside the limits of the official churches for the purpose of teaching what are called "the Mysteries": for imparting to suitable and prepared minds certain truths of human life, certain instructions about divine things, about the things that belong to our peace, about human nature and human destiny, which it was undesirable to publish to the multitude who would but profane those teachings and apply the esoteric knowledge that was communicated to perverse and perhaps to disastrous ends.

These Mysteries were formerly taught, we are told, "on the highest hills and in the lowest valleys," which is merely a figure of speech for saying, first, that they have been taught in circumstances of the greatest seclusion and secrecy, and secondly, that they have been taught in both advanced and simple forms according to the understanding of their disciples. It is, of course, common knowledge that great secret systems of the Mysteries (referred to in our lectures as "noble orders of architecture," *i.e.*, of soul-building) existed in the East, in Chaldea, Assyria, Egypt, Greece, Italy, amongst the Hebrews, amongst Mahommedans and amongst Christians; even among uncivilized African races they are to be found. All the great teachers of humanity, Socrates, Plato, Pythagoras, Moses, Aristotle, Virgil, the author of the Homeric poems, and the great Greek tragedians, along with St. John, St. Paul and innumerable other great names—were initiates of the Sacred Mysteries. The *form* of the teaching communicated has varied considerably

23

from age to age; it has been expressed under
different veils; but since the ultimate truth the
Mysteries aim at teaching is always one and the
same, there has always been taught, and can only be
taught, one and the same doctrine. What that
doctrine was, and still is, we will consider presently
so far as we are able to speak of it, and so far as
Masonry gives expression to it. For the moment
let me merely say that behind all the official religious
systems of the world, and behind all the great moral
movements and developments in the history of
humanity, have stood what St. Paul called the
keepers or " stewards of the Mysteries." From
that source Christianity itself came into the world.
From them originated the great school of Kabalism,
that marvellous system of secret, oral tradition of
the Hebrews, a strong element of which has been
introduced into our Masonic system. From them,
too, also issued many fraternities and orders, such,
for instance, as the great orders of Chivalry and of
the Rosicrucians, and the school of spiritual alchemy.
Lastly, from them too also issued, in the seventeenth
century, modern speculative Freemasonry.

To trace the genesis of the movement, which came
into activity some 250 years ago (our rituals and
ceremonies having been compiled round about the
year 1700), is beyond the purpose of my present
remarks. It may merely be stated that the movement itself incorporated the slender ritual and the
elementary symbolism that, for centuries previously,
had been employed in connection with the mediæval
Building Guilds, but it gave to them a far fuller
meaning and a far wider scope. It has always been

the custom for Trade Guilds, and even for modern
Friendly Societies, to spiritualize their trades, and
to make the tools of their trade point some simple
moral. No trade, perhaps, lends itself more readily
to such treatment than the builder's trade; but
wherever a great industry has flourished, there you
will find traces of that industry becoming allegorized,
and of the allegory being employed for the simple
moral instruction of those who were operative
members of the industry. I am acquainted, for
instance, with an Egyptian ceremonial system, some
5,000 years old, which taught precisely the same
things as Masonry does, but in the terms of ship-
building instead of in the terms of architecture.
But the terms of architecture were employed by
those who originated modern Masonry because they
were ready to hand; because they were in use
among certain trade-guilds then in existence; and
lastly, because they are extremely effective and
significant from the symbolic point of view.

All that I wish to emphasize at this stage is that
our present system is *not* one coming from remote
antiquity : that there is no direct continuity between
us and the Egyptians, or even those ancient Hebrews
who built, in the reign of King Solomon, a certain
Temple at Jerusalem. What *is* extremely ancient
in Freemasonry is the spiritual doctrine concealed
within the architectural phraseology; for this
doctrine is an elementary form of the doctrine that
has been taught in all ages, no matter in what garb
it has been expressed. Our own teaching, for
instance, recognizes Pythagoras as having undergone
numerous initiations in different parts of the world,

and as having attained great eminence in the science.
Now it is perfectly certain that Pythagoras was not
a Mason at all in our present sense of the word;
but it is also perfectly certain that Pythagoras was
a very highly advanced master in the knowledge of
the secret schools of the Mysteries, of whose doctrine
some small portion is enshrined for us in our
Masonic system.

What then was the purpose the framers of our
Masonic system had in view when they compiled
it? To this question you will find no satisfying
answer in ordinary Masonic books. Indeed there
is nothing more dreary and dismal than Masonic
literature and Masonic histories, which are usually
devoted to considering merely unessential matters
relating to the external development of the Craft
and to its antiquarian aspect. They fail entirely
to deal with its vital meaning and essence, a failure
that, in some cases, may be intentional, but that
more often seems due to lack of knowledge and
perception, for the true, inner history of Masonry
has never yet been given forth even to the Craft
itself. There are members of the Craft to whom
it is familiar, and who in due time may feel justified
in gradually making public at any rate some portion
of what is known in interior circles. But ere that
time comes, and that the Craft itself may the better
appreciate what can be told, it is desirable, nay even
necessary, that its own members should make some
effort to realize the meaning of their own institution,
and should display symptoms of earnest desire to
treat it less as a system of archaic and perfunctory
rites, and more as a vital reality capable of entering

into and dominating their lives ; less as a merely pleasant social order, and more as a sacred and serious method of initiation into the profoundest truths of life   It is written that " to him that hath shall be given, and from him that hath not shall be taken away even that which he hath " ; and it remains with the Craft itself to determine by its own action whether it shall enter into its full heritage, or whether, by failing to realize and to safeguard the value of what it possesses, by suffering its own mysteries to be vulgarized and profaned, its organiza- tion will degenerate and pass into disrepute and deserved oblivion, as has been the fate of many secret orders in the past.

There are signs, however, of a well-nigh universal increase of interest, of a genuine desire for knowledge of the spiritual content of our Masonic system, and I am glad to be able to offer to my Brethren some light and imperfect outline of what I conceive to be the true purpose of our work, which may tend to deepen their interest in the work of the Order they belong to, and (what is of more moment still) help to make Masonry for them a vital factor, and a living, serious reality, rather than a mere pleasurable appendage to social life.

To state things briefly, Masonry offers us, in dramatic form and by means of dramatic ceremonial a philosophy of the spiritual life of man and a diagram of the process of regeneration. We shall see presently that that philosophy is not only consistent with the doctrine of every religious system taught outside the ranks of the Order, but that it explains, elucidates and more sharply defines, the

fundamental doctrines common to every religious
system in the world, whether past or present,
whether Christian or non-Christian. The religions
of the world, though all aiming at teaching truth,
express that truth in different ways, and we are more
prone to emphasize the differences than to look for
the correspondences in what they teach. In some
Masonic Lodges the candidate makes his first
entrance to the Lodge room amid the clash of swords
and the sounds of strife, to intimate to him that he
is leaving the confusion and jarring of the religious
sects of the exterior world, and is passing into a
Temple wherein the Brethren dwell together in
unity of thought in regard to the basal truths of
life, truths which can permit of no difference or
schism.

Allied with no external religious system itself,
Masonry is yet a synthesis, a concordat, for men of
every race, of every creed, of every sect, and its
foundation principles being common to them all,
admit of no variation. "As it was in the beginning,
so it is now and ever shall be, into the ages of ages."
Hence it is that every Master of a Lodge is called
upon to swear that no innovation in the body of
Masonry (*i.e.*, in its substantial doctrine) is possible,
since it already contains a minimum, and yet a
sufficiency, of truth which none may add to nor
alter, and from which none may take away ; and
since the Order accords perfect liberty of opinion
to all men, the truths it has to offer are entirely
" free *to* " us according to our capacity to assimilate
them, whilst those to whom they do not appeal,
those who think they can find a more sufficing

philosophy elsewhere, are equally at liberty to be "free *from*" them, and men of honour will find it their duty to withdraw from the Order rather than suffer the harmony of thought that should characterize the Craft to be disturbed by their presence.

The admission of every Mason into the Order is, we are taught, " an emblematical representation of the entrance of all men upon this mortal existence." Let us reflect a little upon these pregnant words. To those deep persistent questionings which present themselves to every thinking mind, What am I? Whence come I? Whither go I?, Masonry offers emphatic and luminous answers. Each of us, it tells us, has come from that mystical " East," the eternal source of all light and life, and our life here is described as being spent in the " West " (that is, in a world which is the antipodes of our original home, and under conditions of existence as far removed from those we came from and to which we are returning, as is West from East in our ordinary computation of space). Hence every Candidate upon admission finds himself, in a state of darkness, in the West of the Lodge. Thereby he is repeating symbolically the incident of his actual birth into this world, which he entered as a blind and helpless babe, and through which in his early years, not knowing whither he was going, after many stumbling and irregular steps, after many deviations from the true path and after many tribulations and adversities incident to human life, he may at length ascend, purified and chastened by experience, to larger life in the eternal East. Hence in the E.A. degree, we ask, " As a Mason, whence come you ? " and the answer, coming from an apprentice (*i.e.*, from the natural man of undeveloped knowledge) is " From the West," since he supposes that his life has originated in this world. But, in the advanced degree of M.M. the answer is that he comes " From the East," for by this time the Mason is supposed to have so enlarged his knowledge as to realize that the primal source of life is not in the " West," not in this world ; that existence upon this planet is but a transitory sojourn, spent in search of " the genuine secrets," the ultimate realities, of life ; and that as the spirit of man must return to God who gave it, so he is now returning from this temporary world of " substituted secrets " to that " East " from which he originally came.

As the admission of every candidate into a Lodge presupposes his prior existence in the world without the Lodge, so our doctrine presupposes that every soul born into this world has lived in, and has come hither from, an anterior state of life. It has lived elsewhere before it entered this world : it will live elsewhere when it passes hence, human life being but a parenthesis in the midst of eternity. But upon entering this world, the soul must needs assume material form ; in other words it takes upon itself a physical body to enable it to enter into relations with the physical world, and to perform the functions appropriate to it in this particular phase of its career. Need I say that the physical form with which we have all been invested by the Creator upon our entrance into this world, and of which we shall all divest ourselves when we leave the Lodge of this life, is represented among us by

our Masonic apron ? This, our body of mortality,
this veil of flesh and blood clothing the inner soul
of us, this is the real " badge of innocence," the
common " bond of friendship," with which the
Great Architect has been pleased to invest us all :
this, the human body, is the badge which is " older
and nobler than that of any other Order in
existence " : and though it be but a body of humiliation compared with that body of incorruption which
is the promised inheritance of him who endures to
the end, let us never forget that if we never do
anything to disgrace the badge of flesh with which
God has endowed each of us, that badge will
never disgrace us.

Brethren, I charge you to regard your apron as
one of the most precious and speaking symbols our
Order has to give you. Remember that when you
first wore it it was a piece of pure white lambskin ;
an emblem of that purity and innocence which we
always associate with the lamb and with the new-
born child. Remember that you first wore it with
the flap raised, it being thus a five-cornered badge,
indicating the five senses, by means of which we
enter into relations with the material world around
us (our " five points of fellowship " with the material
world), but indicating also by the triangular portion
above, in conjunction with the quadrangular portion
below, that man's nature is a combination of soul
and body ; the three-sided emblem at the top added
to the four-sided emblem beneath making seven,
the perfect number ; for, as it is written in an
ancient Hebrew doctrine with which Masonry is
closely allied, " God blessed and loved the number

seven more than all things under His throne," by
which is meant that man, the seven-fold being, is
the most cherished of all the Creator's works. And
hence also it is that the Lodge has seven principal
officers, and that a Lodge, to be perfect, requires
the presence of seven brethren ; though the deeper
meaning of this phrase is that the individual man,
in virtue of his seven-fold constitution, *in himself*
constitutes the " perfect Lodge," if he will but
know himself and analyse his own nature aright.

To each of us also from our birth have been given
three lesser lights, by which the Lodge within
ourselves may be illumined. For the " sun "
symbolizes our spiritual consciousness, the higher
aspirations and emotions of the soul ; the " moon "
betokens our reasoning or intellectual faculties,
which (as the moon reflects the light of the sun)
should reflect the light coming from the higher
spiritual faculty and transmit it into our daily
conduct ; whilst " the Master of the Lodge " is a
symbolical phrase denoting the will-power of man,
which should enable him to be master of his own
life, to control his own actions and keep down the
impulses of his lower nature, even as the stroke of
the Master's gavel controls the Lodge and calls to
order and obedience the Brethren under his direction. By the assistance of these lesser lights within
us, a man is enabled to perceive what is, again
symbolically, called the " form of the Lodge," *i.e.*,
the way in which his own human nature has been
composed and constituted, the length, breadth,
height and depth of his own being. By their help,
too, he will perceive that he himself, his body and

his soul, are " holy ground," upon which he should build the altar of his own spiritual life, an altar which he should suffer no " iron tool," no debasing habit of thought or conduct, to defile. By them, too, he will perceive how Wisdom, Strength and Beauty have been employed by the Creator, like three grand supporting pillars, in the structure of his own organism. And by these finally he will discern how that there is a mystical " ladder of many rounds or staves," *i.e.*, that there are innumerable paths or methods by means of which men are led upwards to the spiritual Light encircling us all, and in which we live and move and have our being, but that of the three principal methods, the greatest of these, the one that comprehends them all and brings us nearest heaven, is Love, in the full exercise of which God-like virtue a Mason reaches the summit of his profession; that summit being God Himself, whose name *is* Love.

I cannot too strongly impress upon you, Brethren, the fact that, throughout our rituals and our lectures, the references made to the Lodge are *not* to the building in which we meet. That building itself is intended to be but a symbol, a veil of allegory concealing something else. " Know ye not " says the great initiate St. Paul, " that *ye* are the temples of the Most High; and that the Spirit of God dwelleth in *you* ? " The real Lodge referred to throughout our rituals is our own individual personalities, and if we interpret our doctrine in the light of this fact we shall find that it reveals an entirely new aspect of the purpose of our Craft.

It is after investment with the apron that the

initiate is placed in the N.E. corner. Thereby he is intended to learn that at his birth into this world the foundation-stone of his spiritual life was duly and truly laid and implanted within himself; and he is charged to develop it; to create a super-structure upon it. Two paths are open to him at this stage, a path of light and a path of darkness; a path of good and a path of evil. The N.E. corner is the symbolical dividing place between the two. In symbolical language, the N. always signifies the place of imperfection and undevelopment; in olden times the bodies of suicides, reprobates and unbap-tized children were always buried in the north or sunless side of a churchyard. The seat of the junior members of the Craft is allotted to the north, for, symbolically, it represents the condition of the spiritually unenlightened man; the novice in whom the spiritual light latent within him has not yet risen above the horizon of consciousness and dispersed the clouds of material interests and the impulses of the lower and merely sensual life. The initiate placed in the N.E. corner is intended to see, then, that on the one side of him is the path that leads to the perpetual light of the East, into which he is encouraged to proceed, and that on the other is that of spiritual obscurity and ignorance into which it is possible for him to remain or relapse. It is a parable of the dual paths of life open to each one of us; on the one hand the path of selfishness, material desires and sensual indulgence, of intellec-tual blindness and moral stagnation; on the other the path of moral and spiritual progress, in pursuing which one may decorate and adorn the Lodge within him with the ornaments and jewels of grace and with the invaluable furniture of true knowledge, and which he may dedicate, in all his actions, to the service of God and of his fellow men And mark that of those jewels some are said to be moveable and transferable, because when displayed in our own lives and natures their influence becomes transferred and communicated to others and helps to uplift and sweeten the lives of our fellows ; whilst some are immoveable because they are permanently fixed and planted in the roots of our own being, and are indeed the raw material which has been entrusted to us to work out of chaos and roughness into due and true form.

The Ceremony of our first degree, then, is a swift and comprehensive portrayal of the entrance of all men into, first, physical life, and second, into spiritual life ; and as we extend congratulations when a child is born into the world, so also we receive with acclamation the candidate for Masonry who, symbolically, is seeking for spiritual re-birth ; and herein we emulate what is written of the joy that exists among the angels of heaven over every sinner who repents and turns towards the light. The first degree is also eminently the degree of preparation, of self-discipline and purification. It corresponds with that symbolical cleansing accorded in the sacrament of Baptism, which, in the churches, is, so to speak, the first degree in the religious life ; and which is administered, appropriately, at the font, near the entrance of the church, even as the act itself takes place at the entrance of the spiritual career. For to all of us such initial cleansing and purifying is necessary. As has been beautifully written by a fellow-worker in the Craft:—

> " 'Tis scarcely true that souls come naked down
> To take abode up in this earthly town,
> Or naked pass, of all they wear denied.
> We enter slipshod and with clothes awry,
> And we take with us much that by-and-by
> May prove no easy task to put aside.
>
> Cleanse, therefore, that which round about us clings,
> We pray Thee, Master, ere Thy sacred halls
> We enter. Strip us of redundant things,
> And meetly clothe us in pontificals.*

In the schools of the Mysteries, when aspirants for the higher life were wont to quit the outer world and enter temples or sanctuaries of initiation, prolonged periods were allotted to the practical achievement of what is briefly summarized in our first degree. We are told seven or more years was the normal period, though less sufficed in worthy cases. The most severe tests of discipline, of purity, of self-balance were required before a neophyte was permitted to pass forward, and a reminiscence of these tests of fitness is preserved in our own working by the conducting of the candidate to the two wardens, and submitting him to a merely formal trial of efficiency. For it is impossible to-day, as it was impossible in ancient times, for a man to reach the heights of moral perfection and spiritual consciousness which were then, and are now, the goal and aim of all the schools of the Mysteries and all the secret orders, without purification and trial. Complete stainlessness of body, utter purity of

Strange Houses of Sleep by A. E. Waite.

mind, are absolute essentials to the attainment of things of great and final moment. " Who " says the Psalmist (and remember that the Psalms were the sacred hymns used in the Hebrew Mysteries), " Who will go up to the hill of the Lord, and ascend to His holy place ? Even he that hath clean hands and a pure heart " ; whence it comes that we wear white gloves and aprons as emblems that we have purified our hearts and washed our hands in innocency. So also our Patron Saint (St. John) teaches, " He who hath this hope in him purifieth himself, even as He (*i.e.*, the Master whom he is seeking) is pure." For he who is not pure in body and mind : he who is enslaved by passions and desires, or by bondage to the material interests of this world, is, by the very fact of his uncleanness, prevented from passing on. Nothing unclean or that defileth a man, we are told, can enter into the kingdom ; and, therefore, our candidates are told that if they have " money or metals about them " ; if, that is, they are subject to any physical attraction or mental defilement, their real initiation into the higher things, of which our ceremony is but a dramatic symbol, must be deferred and repeated again and again until they are cleansed and fitted to pass on.

After purification come contemplation and enlightenment, which are the special subjects of the second degree. Aforetime the candidate for the Mysteries, after protracted discipline and purification enabling his mind to acquire complete control over his passions and his lower physical nature, was advanced, as he may advance himself to-day, to the study of his more interior faculties, to

37

understand the science of the human soul, and to
trace these faculties in their development from their
elementary stage until he realizes that they connect
with, and terminate in, the Divine itself.   The
secrets of his mental nature and the principles of
intellectual life became at this stage gradually
unfolded to his view. You will thus perceive,
Brethren, that the F.C. degree, sometimes regarded
by us as a somewhat uninteresting one, typifies in
reality a long course of personal development
requiring the most profound knowledge of the
mental and psychical side of our nature.   It involves
not merely the cleansing and control of the mind, but
a full comprehension of our inner constitution, of the
more hidden mysteries of our nature and of spiritual
psychology.   In this degree it is that our attention
is called to the fact that the Mason who has attained
proficiency in this grade has been enabled to discover
a sacred symbol, placed in the centre of the building,
and alluding to the G.G.O.T.U. Doubtless we have
often asked ourselves what that phrase and what
that symbol imply.   Need I repeat that the building
alluded to is not the edifice we meet in, but is our
own selves, and that the sacred symbol at the
centre of the roof and of the floor of this outward
temple is but symbolic of that which exists at the
centre of ourselves, and which was spoken of by the
Christian Master when He proclaimed that " the
kingdom of heaven is within you " ; that at the
depths of our own being, concealed beneath the
heavy veils of the sensual, lower nature, there
resides that vital and immortal principle, which is
said to " allude to " the G.G. because it is nothing

other than a spark of God Himself immanent within us. Over the old temples of the Mysteries was written the injunction "Man, know thyself, and thou shalt know the universe and God." Happy then is the Mason who has so far purified and developed his own nature as to realize in its fulness the meaning of the "sacred symbol" of the second degree, and found God present not outside but within himself. But in order to find the "perfect points of entrance" to this secret (and we are told elsewhere that "straight is the way and narrow the gate, and few there be that find it") emphasis again is laid in our teaching upon the necessity of complete moral rectitude, of utter exactness of thought, word and action, as exemplified by rigid observance of the symbolic principles of the square, level and plumb-rule.

Here again the symbolism of our work becomes extremely profound and interesting. He who desires to rise to the heights of his own being must first crush and crucify his own lower nature and inclinations; he must perforce tread what elsewhere is described as the way of the Cross; and that Cross is indicated by the conjunction of those working tools (which when united form a cross); and that "way" is involved in the scrupulous performance of all that we know those working tools signify. By perfecting his conduct, by struggles against his own natural propensities, the candidate is working the rough ashlar of his own nature into the perfect cube, and I would ask you to observe also that the cube itself contains a secret, for unfolded, it itself denotes and takes the form of the cross.

The inward development which the second degree symbolizes is typified by the lowering of the triangular flap of the apron upon the rectangular portion below. This is equivalent to the rite of Confirmation in the Christian Churches. It denotes " the progress we have made in the science," or in other words it indicates that the higher nature of the man, symbolized by the trinity of spirit, has descended into and is now permeating his lower nature. Hitherto, in his state of ignorance and moral blindness, the spiritual part of his nature has, as it were, but hovered above him ; he has been unconscious of its presence in his constitution ; but now, having realized its existence, the day-spring from on high has visited him, and the nobler part of him descends into his lower nature, illuminating and enriching it.

Now the man who so develops himself, speedily becomes more conscious of the difficulties of his task, more sensitive to the obstacles the life of the outer world places in the way of the spiritual life. But he is taught to persist with fortitude and with prudence, to develop the highest within him with " fervency and zeal." Upon self-scrutiny, too, *i.e.,* upon entering into that " porchway " of contemplation which like a winding staircase leads inward to the Holy of Holies within himself, he realizes that difficulties and obstacles placed in his way are utilised by the Eternal Wisdom as the necessary means of developing the latent and potential good in him, and that as the rough ashlar can only be squared and perfected by chipping and polishing, so he also can be made perfect only by toil and by suffering. He sees that difficulty, adversity and persecution serve a beneficent purpose. These are his "wages": and he learns to accept them "without scruple and without diffidence, knowing that he is justly entitled to them, and from the confidence he has in the integrity" of that Employer who has sent him into this far-off world to prepare the materials for building the temple of the heavenly city. And so, as the sign peculiar to the degree suggests, he endeavours to examine and lay bare his heart, to cast away all impurity from it, and he stands, like Joshua, praying that the light of day may be extended to him until he has accomplished the overthrow of his own inward enemies and of every obstacle to his complete development.

The aspirant who attains proficiency in the work of self-perfecting to which the F.C. grade alludes, has passed away from the N. side of the Lodge, the side of darkness and imperfection; and now stands on the S.E. side in the meridian sunlight of moral illumination (so far as the natural man may possess it), but yet still far removed from that fuller realization of himself and of the mysteries of his own nature which it is possible for the spiritual adept or Master Mason to attain. Before that attainment is reached there remains for him "that last and greatest trial" by which alone he can enter into the great consolations and make acquaintance with the supreme realities of existence. In the places where the great Mysteries have always been taught, what is ceremonially performed in our third degree is no mere symbolical representation as with us, but an actual, vital experience of a most severe

41

character : one the nature of which can hardly be made intelligible, or even credible, to those unfamiliar with the subject. I refrain, therefore, from more than mere mention of it, observing only that it is one not involving physical death, and in this respect only is our ceremony in accord with the experience symbolized. For if you follow closely the raising ceremony, although distinct reference to the death of the body is made, yet such death is obviously intended to be merely symbolical of another kind of death, since the candidate is eventually restored to his former worldly circumstances and material comforts, and his earthly Masonic career is not represented as coming to a close at this stage. All that has happened in the third degree is that he has symbolically passed through a great and striking change : a rebirth, or regeneration of his whole nature. He has been " sown a corruptible body " ; and in virtue of the self-discipline and self-development he has undergone, there has been raised in him " an incorruptible body," and death has been swallowed up in the victory he has attained over himself. I sometimes fear that the too conspicuous display of the emblems and trappings of mortality in our Lodges is apt to create the false impression that the death to which the third degree alludes is the mere physical change that awaits all men. But a far deeper meaning is intended. The Mason who knows his science knows that the death of the body is only a natural transition of which he need have no dread whatever ; he knows also that when the due time for it arrives, that transition will be a welcome respite from the bondage of this world, from his prison-like husk of mortality, and from the daily burdens incident to existence in this lower plane of life. All that he fears is that when the time comes, he may not be free from those " stains of falsehood and dishonour," those imperfections of his own nature, that may delay his after-progress. No ! the death to which Masonry alludes, using the analogy of bodily death and under the veil of a reference to it, is that death-in-life to a man's own lower self which St. Paul referred to when he protested " I die daily." It is over the grave, not of one's dead body but of one's lower self, that the aspirant must walk before attaining to the heights. What is meant is that complete self-sacrifice and self-crucifixion which, as all religions teach, are essential before the soul can be raised in glory " from a figurative death to a reunion with the companions of its former toils " both here and in the unseen world. The perfect cube must pass through the metamorphosis of the Cross. The soul must voluntarily and consciously pass through a state of utter helplessness from which no earthly hand can rescue it, and in trying to raise him from which the grip of any succouring human hand will prove but a slip : until at length Divine Help itself descends from the Throne above and, with the " lion's grip " of almighty power, raises the faithful and regenerated soul to union with itself in an embrace of reconciliation and at-one-ment.

In all the schools of the Mysteries, as well as in all the great religions of the world, the attainment of the spiritual goal just described is enacted or taught under the veil of a tragic episode analogous to that of our third degree; and in each there is a Master whose death the aspirant is instructed he must imitate in his own person. In Masonry that prototype is Hiram Abiff: but it must be made clear that there is no historical basis whatever for the legendary account of Hiram's death. The entire story is symbolical and was purposely invented for the symbolical purposes of our teaching. If you examine it closely you will perceive how obvious the correspondence is between this story and the story of the death of the Christian Master related in the Gospels; and it is needless to say that the Mason who realizes the meaning of the latter will comprehend the former and the veiled allusion that is implied. In the one case the Master is crucified between the two thieves; in the other he is done to death between two villains. In the one case appear the penitent and the impenitent thief; in the other we have the conspirators who make a voluntary confession of their guilt and were pardoned, and the others who were found guilty and put to death; whilst the moral and spiritual lessons deducible from the stories correspond. As every Christian is taught that in his own life he must imitate the life and death of Christ, so every Mason is " made to represent one of the brightest characters recorded in our annals "; but as the annals of Masonry are contained in the volume of the Sacred Law and not elsewhere, it is easy to see who the character is who is alluded to. As that great authority and initiate of the Mysteries, St. Paul, taught, we can only attain to the Master's resurrection by " being made conformable unto His death," and we " must

die with Him if we are to be raised like Him ":
and it is in virtue of that conformity, in virtue of
being individually made to imitate the Grand
Master in His death, that we are made worthy of
certain " points of fellowship " with Him : for the
" five points of fellowship " of the third degree are
the five wounds of Christ   The three years' ministry
of the Christian Master ended with His death and,
these refer to the three degrees of the Craft which
also end in the mystical death of the Masonic
candidate and his subsequent raising or resurrection.

The name Hiram Abiff signifies in Hebrew " the
teacher (Guru, or enlightened one) from the
Father " : a fact which may help you still further
to recognize the concealed purpose of the teaching.
Under the name of Hiram, then, and beneath a veil
of allegory, we see an allusion to another Master ;
and it is this Master, this Elder Brother who is
alluded to in our lectures, whose " character we
preserve, whether absent or present," *i.e.*, whether
He is present to our minds or no, and in regard to
whom we " adopt the excellent principle, silence,"
lest at any time there should be among us trained
in some other than the Christian Faith, and to whom
on that account the mention of the Christian
Master's name might possibly prove an offence or
provoke contention.

To typify the advance by the candidate at this stage
of his development, the apron here assumes greater
elaborateness. It is garnished with a light blue
border and rosettes, indicating that a higher than
the natural light now permeates his being and
radiates from his person, and that the wilderness

of the natural man is now blossoming as the rose, in the flowers and graces incident to his regenerated nature; whilst upon either side of the apron are seen two columns of light descending from above, streaming into the depths of his whole being, and terminating in the seven-fold tassels which typify the seven-fold prismatic spectrum of the supernal Light. He is now lord of himself; the true Master-Mason; able to govern that lodge which is within himself; and as he has passed through the three degrees of purifying and self-perfecting, and squared, levelled, and harmonized his triple nature of body, soul and spirit, he also wears, on attaining Mastership, the triple *Tau*; which comprises the form of a level, but is also the Hebrew form of the Cross; the three crosses upon the apron thus corresponding with the three crosses of Calvary.

To sum up the import of the teaching of the three degrees, it is clear, therefore, that from grade to grade the candidate is being led from an old to an entirely new quality of life. He begins his Masonic career as the natural man; he ends it by becoming through its discipline, a regenerated perfected man. To attain this transmutation, this metamorphosis of himself, he is taught first to purify and subdue his sensual nature; then to purify and develop his mental nature; and finally, by utter surrender of his old life and losing his soul to save it, he rises from the dead a Master, a just man made perfect, with larger consciousness and faculties, an efficient instrument for use by the Great Architect in His plan of rebuilding the Temple of fallen humanity, and capable of initiating and advancing other men to a participation in the same great work.

This—the evolution of man into superman—was always the purpose of the ancient Mysteries, and the real purpose of modern Masonry is, not the social and charitable purposes to which so much attention is paid, but the expediting of the spiritual evolution of those who aspire to perfect their own nature and transform it into a more god-like quality. And this is a definite science, a royal art, which it is possible for each of us to put into practice; whilst to join the Craft for any other purpose than to study and pursue this science is to misunderstand its meaning. Hence it is that no one should apply to enter Masonry unless from the deepest promptings of his own heart, as it hungers for light upon the problem of its own nature. We are all imperfect beings, conscious of something lacking to us that would make us what, in our best moments, we fain would be. What is that which is lacking to us? "What is that which is lost?" And the answer is "The genuine secrets of a Master Mason," the true knowledge of ourselves, the conscious realization of our divine potentialities.

The very essence of the Masonic doctrine is that all men in this world are in search of something in their own nature which they have lost, but that with proper instruction and by their own patience and industry they may hope to find. Its philosophy implies that this temporal world is the antipodes of another and more real world from which we originally came and to which we may accelerate our return by such a course of self-knowledge and self-discipline

47

as our teaching inculcates. It implies that this present world is the place where the symbolic stones and timber are being prepared " so far off " from that mystical Jerusalem where one day they will be found put together and, collectively, to constitute that Temple which even now is being built without hands and without the noise or help of metal tools. And this world, therefore, being but a transient temporary one for us, it is necessarily one of shadows, images and merely " substituted secrets," until such time as being raised not merely symbolically but actually, in character and knowledge and consciousness, to the sublime degree of Master Mason, we fit ourselves to learn something of the " genuine secrets," something of the living realities, that lurk and live in concealment behind the outward show of things. All human life, having originated in the mystical " East " and journeyed into this world which, with us, is the " West," must return again to its source. To quote again the verse of the Brother I have already cited :—

" From East to West the soul her journey takes ;
At many bitter founts her fever slakes ;
Halts at strange taverns by the way to feast,
Resumes her load, and painful progress makes
        Back to the East."

Masonry, by means of a series of dramatic representations, is intended to furnish those who care to discover its purport and to take advantage of the hints it throws out in allegorical form, with an example and with instructions by which our return to the " East " may be accelerated. It refers to no architecture of a mundane kind, but to the architecture of the soul's life. It is not in itself a religion; but rather a dramatized and intensified form of religious processes inculcated by every religious system in the world. For there is no religion but teaches the lesson of the necessity of bodily purification of our first degree; none but emphasizes that of the second degree, that mental, moral and spiritual developments are essential and will lead to the discovery of a certain secret centre " where truth abides in fulness," and that that centre is a " point within a circle " of our own nature from which no man or Mason can ever err, for it is the divine kingdom latent within us all, into which we have as yet failed to enter. And there is none but insists upon the supreme lesson of self-sacrifice and mystical death to the things of this world so graphically portrayed in our third degree; none but indicates that in that hour of greatest darkness the light of the primal divine spark within us is never wholly extinguished, and that by loyalty to that light, by patience and by perseverance, time and circumstances will restore to us the " genuine secrets," the ultimate truths and realities of our own nature. We are here, Masonry teaches, as it were in captivity, by the waters of Babylon and in a strange land; and our doctrine truly tells us that the richest harmonies of this life are as nothing in comparison with the songs of Zion; and that, even when we are installed into the highest eminences this world or the Craft may offer, it were better that our right hand should forget its cunning and that we should fling the illusory treasures of this transitory world behind

our backs, than in all our doings fail to remember
the Jerusalem that lies beyond.

Our teaching is purposely veiled in allegory and
symbol and its deeper import does not appear upon
the surface of the ritual itself. This is partly in
correspondence with human life itself and the world
we live in, which are themselves but allegories and
symbols of another life and the veils of another
world; and partly intentional also, so that only
those who have reverent and understanding minds
may penetrate into the more hidden meaning of the
doctrine of the Craft. The deeper secrets in
Masonry, like the deeper secrets of life, are heavily
veiled; are closely hidden. They exist concealed
beneath a great reservation; but whoso knows
anything of them knows also that they are " many
and valuable," and that they are disclosed only to
those who act upon the hint given in our lectures,
" Seek and ye shall find; ask and ye shall have;
knock and it shall be opened unto you." The
search may be long and difficult, but great things are
not acquired without effort and search; but it may
be affirmed that to the candidate who is " properly
prepared " (in a much fuller sense than we conven-
tionally attach to that expression) there are doors
leading from the Craft that, when knocked, will
assuredly open and admit him to places and to
knowledge he at present recks little of. For him,
too, who would enter upon the greater initiations,
the same rule applies as that which was symbolically
represented upon his first entrance into the Order,
but this time it will no longer be a symbol, but a
realistic fact. He will find, I mean, that a drawn

sword is always threatening in front of him, and that a cable-tow is still around his neck. Danger, indeed, awaits the candidate who would rush precipitately and in a state of moral unfitness into the deeper mysteries of his being, which are indeed " serious, solemn and awful " ; but, on the other hand, for him who has once entered upon the path of light it is moral suicide to turn back.

And now, Brethren, to bring to an end this brief and imperfect survey of the deeper meaning and purposes of our Craft, I pray that what is now spoken may help to prove to some of you a further restoration to that light which is, at all times, the predominant wish of our hearts. It rests with ourselves whether Masonry remains for us what upon its outward and superficial side appears to be merely a series of symbolic rites, or whether we allow those symbols to pass into our lives and become realities therein. Whatever formalities we may have gone through in connection with our admission into the Order, we cannot be said to have been " regularly initiated " into Masonry so long as we regard the Craft as merely an incident of social life and treat its ceremonies as but rites of an archaic and perfunctory nature. The Craft, as I have already suggested, was given out to the world, from more secret sources still, as a great experiment and means of grace, and as a great opportunity for those who cared to avail themselves of what is little known and little taught outside certain sanctuaries of concealment. It was intended to furnish forth an epitome or synopsis, in dramatic form, of the spiritual regeneration of man ; and to throw out

hints and suggestions that might lead those capable
of discerning its deeper purpose and symbolism into
still deeper initiations than the merely superficial
ones enacted in our Lodges.   For, as on the external
side of the Order we may be called to occupy
positions of honour and office in the Provincial
Grand Lodge, or may enter other Masonic grades
outside the Craft, so also upon its internal side there
are eminences to which we may be called that,
whilst offering us no social distinction and no
visible advancement, are yet really the true prizes,
the most valuable attainments, of Masonic desire.
To this goal all may attain who truly seek to do so
and who prepare the way for themselves by appro-
priating the truths lying beneath the superficial
allegory and the symbolic veils of the Craft teaching.
And since there seems to-day a genuine and wide-
spread desire on the part of many members of the
Order to enter into a fuller understanding of what
the Order itself conceals rather than reveals, I feel
I should not be discharging my duties as a Master
in the Craft did I not take advantage of that position
to share with them some measure at least of what I
have been able to glean for myself.

But, finally, I must ask you to remember that,
in accordance with the general design of our system,
every Master of a Lodge is but a symbol and a
substitution, and that behind him, and behind all
other the grand officers of the Masonic hierarchy,
there stands the " Great White Head," the " Great
Initiator " and Grand Master of all true Masons
throughout the Universe, whether members of our
Craft or not.   To whom let us all bow in gratitude

for the invaluable gift accorded to us in this our *The* Order; and to whose protection, and to whose *Deeper* enlightening guidance into its deeper mysteries, I *Sym-* commend you all. *bolism of* *Masonry*

Chapter II.

MASONRY AS A PHILOSOPHY

SIGNS are not wanting that a higher Masonic consciousness is awakening in the Craft. Members of the Order are gradually, and here and there, becoming alive to the fact that much more than meets the eye and ear lies beneath the surface of Masonic doctrine and symbols. They are beginning to think for themselves instead of taking the face-value of things for granted, and, as their thought develops, facts that previously remained unperceived assume prominence and significance. They discern the Masonic system to be something deeper than a code of elementary morality such as all men are expected to observe whether formally Masons or not. They reflect that the phenomenal growth of the Craft is scarcely accountable for upon the supposition that modern speculative Masonry perpetuates nothing more than the private associations that once existed in connection with the operative builders' trade. They recognize that there can be no peculiar virtue or interest in continuing to imitate the customs of ancient trade-guilds for the mere sake of so doing; or of keeping on foot a costly organization for teaching men the elementary symbolism of a few building tools, supplemented by a considerable amount of social conviviality. Upon a little thought it becomes pretty obvious that our Third Degree and the great central legend that forms the climax of the Craft system cannot have, and can never have had, any direct or practical bearing upon, or connection with, the trade of the operative mason. It may be urged that we have our great charity system and that the social side of our proceedings is a valuable and humanizing asset. Granted, but other people and other societies are philanthropic and social as well as we ; and a secret society is not necessary to promote such ends, which are merely supplemental to the original purpose of the Order. The discernment of such facts as these, then, suggests to us that the Craft has not yet entered into the full heritage of understanding its own system and that side-matters connected with Masonry which we have long emphasized so strongly, valuable in their own way as they are, are not after all the primary and proper work of the Order. The work of the Order is to initiate into certain secrets and mysteries, and obviously if the Order fails to expound its own secrets and mysteries and so to confer real initiations as distinguished from passing candidates through certain formal ceremonies, it is not fulfilling its original purpose whatever other incidental good it may be doing.

Now as these facts are the basis upon which this lecture proceeds, let me at the outset make my first point by stating that as the progress in the Craft of every Brother admitted into its ranks is by gradual, successive stages, in like manner the understanding of the Masonic system and doctrine is also a matter of gradual development. Stated in the simplest terms possible, the theory of Masonic progress is that every Member admitted to the Order enters in a state of darkness and ignorance as to what Masonry teaches, and that later on he is supposed to be brought to light and knowledge.

Putting it in other terms, he enters the Craft symbolically as a rough ashlar and it is his business so to develop both his character and his understanding that ultimately, in virtue of what he has learned and practised, he may be as a finished and perfect cube.

Now the understanding of the Masonic scheme tends to develop upon precisely similar lines. Its meaning is not discernible all at once, and unless our minds are properly prepared and our understandings carefully trained, they are unlikely ever to participate in the real secrets and mysteries of Masonry at all, however often we may watch the performance of external ceremonial or however proficient we may be in memorizing the rituals and instruction lectures. The first stage, the first conception of what Masonry involves, is concerned merely with the surface-value of the doctrine; with an acquaintance with the literal side of the imparted knowledge which we all obtain upon entering the Craft. Beyond this stage the vast majority of Masons, it is to be feared, never passes. This is the stage of knowledge in which the Craft is regarded as a social, semi-public, semi-secret community to which it is agreeable and advantageous to belong for sociable or even for ulterior purposes; in which the goal of the Mason's ambition is to attain office and high preferment and to wear a breastful of decorations; in which he takes a literal, superficial and historic view of the subject-matter of the doctrine; in which ability to perform the ceremonial work with dignity and effectiveness and to know the instruction catechisms by heart, so that not a syllable is wrongly rendered, is deemed the height of Masonic proficiency; and where, after discharging these functions with a certain degree of credit, his idea is often to have the Lodge closed as speedily as may be and get away to the relaxation of the festive board.

Now all these things belong to what may be called the very rough-ashlar stage of the Masonic conception. I am not, of course, alluding to any individual Mason. I confess frankly to having come within this category myself, and I think we may agree that we have all passed through the phase I have described, for the simple reason that we knew nothing better and had no one able to teach us something better. Let us not complain. If we look back upon the progress of the Craft during the last 150 years we cannot but congratulate ourselves upon the enormous, if gradual, strides made in Masonic progress and decorum even in the rough-ashlar stage of our conception of it. Any-one familiar with the records of old Lodges will have been brought into close touch with times when almost every element of reverence and dignity seems to have been lacking. Lodges were held in the public rooms of taverns. Whatever official furniture decorated these primitive temples, quart-pots and " churchwardens " figured largely among the unauthorized equipment. In one of the great London galleries there hangs a famous picture called " Night " by the great artist and moralist of his age, Hogarth. His purpose was to depict a charac-teristic night-scene in the streets of London as they appeared in his time. Among the typical specimens of depravity haunting those ill-lit streets, the great artist has held up to the derision of all time the figure of a Freemason staggering home drunk, still wearing his apron and being assisted by the tyler of the Lodge. No true Mason can regard this picture without a burning sense of shame, and without registering a resolution to redeem the Craft from this stigma. We have, I hope, got past such things as these. We have awakened to some sense of dignity and self-reverence. The Craft is well governed by its higher authorities, and individual Lodges take a pride in providing proper temples and in conducting their assemblies with due regard to the solemnity of Masonic doctrine. May the Order never relapse into the primitive and chaotic condition from which it has emerged.

But this improvement in matters of external deportment, great and welcome as it is, is not enough. To prevent the Order settling down into a state of self-satisfaction with its social privileges and the agreeableness of friendly intercourse among its members ; to prevent its making its claims to being a system of knowledge and science as perfunctory and little onerous as possible, the improvement I have spoken of must be attended (and I believe is destined to be attended) by an awakening to the deep significance of the Craft's internal purposes. And since I have referred to what I have termed the " rough - ashlar " conception of that purpose you have the right to ask me now to state that loftier conception which may be regarded, in comparison, as the " perfect cube." The answer to this enquiry I shall not attempt to state in so many words. I invite you to regard this whole lecture as an indication of what that answer must be. To some extent I endeavoured to formulate that answer upon a previous occasion, but whilst I then entered rather into the details and minutiæ of the Craft system and symbols, I shall treat the subject now upon broader lines and deal with Masonry in its wider and more philosophic aspect. I said upon that occasion—and I must repeat it now—that in its broad and more vital doctrine Masonry was essentially a philosophic and religious system expressed in dramatic ceremonial. It is a system intended to supply answers to the three great questions that press so inexorably upon the attention of every thoughtful man and that are the subject around which all religions and all philosophies move : What am I ? Whence come I ? Whither go I ? It is a truism to say that in our quieter and more serious moments we all feel the need of some reliable answer to these questions. Light upon them is " the predominant wish of our hearts " ; and upon such light as we can obtain, whether from Masonry or elsewhere, depends our philosophy of life and the rule of conduct by which we regulate our life. In a larger sense, then, than our conventional limited one, the Masonic candidate is presumed to enter the Order in search of light upon these problems ; light that he is presumed not to have succeeded in finding elsewhere. If his candidature is actuated by any motive other than a genuine desire for knowledge upon *these* problems, which beyond all others are vital to his peace, and by a sincere wish to render himself, by the help of that knowledge, serviceable to his fellow-creatures, then his candidature is less than a worthy one. The reason why no man should be solicited to join the Order is that in regard to these matters of sacred and momentous import, the first springs of impulse *must* originate within the postulant himself; the first place of his preparation must ever be in his own heart, and it is to the cry and knocking of his inward need, and for no less a motive, that—in theory, though scarcely in practice—the door to the Mysteries is opened and the seeker enters in and finds help. At another stage of his symbolical progress the candidate learns from his superior brethren, that they, along with himself, are in search of something that is lost and which they have hopes of finding. And it is here that the great motive of this and of all quests, as well as the clue to the real purpose of Masonry, appears prominently and is stated in emphatic terms. Masonry is the quest after something that has been lost. Now what is it that has been lost? Consider the matter thus. Why should we, or the world at large, require systems of religion and philosophy at all? What is the motive and reason for the existence of a Masonic Order and of many other Orders of Initiation, both of the past and the present? Why should they exist at all? I might reduce the matter to the compass of a small and personal point by asking why have you come to hear this lecture, and why should I have been striving for many years to acquire the information that enables me to give it?—if it be not the fact,—as indeed it is, that every man in his reflective moments realizes the sense of some element of his own being having become lost ; that he is conscious, if he be honest with himself, of the sense of moral imperfection, of ignorance, of restricted knowledge about himself and his surroundings; that he is aware, in short, of some radical deficiency in his constitution, which, were it but found and made good, would satisfy this craving for information, for completeness and perfection, would " lead him from darkness to light," and would put him beyond ignorance and beyond the touch of the many ills that flesh is heir to. The point is too obvious to need pressing further, and the answer to it is to be found by a reference to a great doctrine that forms the philosophic basis of all systems of religion, and all the great systems of the Mysteries and of Initiation of antiquity, *viz.*, that which is popularly known as the Fall of Man. However we may choose to regard this event—and throughout the history of the human race it has been taught in innumerable ways and in all manner of parables, allegories, myths and legends—its sole and single meaning is that humanity as a whole has fallen away from its original parent-source and place; that from being imbedded in the eternal centre of life man has become projected to the circumference; and that in this present world of ours he is undergoing a period of restriction, of ignorance, of discipline and experience, that shall ultimately fit him to return to the centre whence he came and to which he properly belongs. " Paradise Lost " is the real theme of Masonry no less than of Milton, as it is also of all the ancient systems of the Mysteries. The Masonic doctrine focuses and

emphasizes the fact and the sense of this loss.
Beneath a veil of allegory describing the intention
to build a certain temple that could not be finished
because of an untimely disaster, Masonry implies
that Humanity is the real temple whose building
became obstructed, and that we, who are both the
craftsmen and the building materials of what was
intended to be an unparalleled structure, are, owing
to a certain unhappy event, living here in this
world in conditions where the genuine and full
secrets of our nature are, for the time being, lost
to us; where the full powers of the soul of man are
curtailed by the limitations of physical life; and
where, during our apprenticeship of probation and
discipline, we have to put up with the substituted
knowledge derivable through our limited and very
fallible senses.

But, whilst Masonry emphasizes this great truth,
it indicates also—and this is its great virtue and real
purpose—the method by which we may regain that
which is lost to us. It holds out the great promise
that, with divine assistance and by our own industry,
the genuine realities of which we at present possess
but the imperfect shadows shall be restored to us,
and that patience and perseverance will eventually
entitle every worthy man to a participation in them.
This large subject is mirrored in miniature in the
Craft ceremonial. The East of the Lodge is the
symbolic centre; the source of all light; the place
of the throne of the Master of all life. The West,
the place of the disappearing sun, is this world of
imperfection and darkness from which the divine
spiritual light is in large measure withdrawn and

only shines by reflection. The ceremonies through which the candidate passes are symbolic of the stages of progress that every man—whether a formal member of the Craft or not—may make by way of self-purification and self-building, until he at length lies dead to his present natural self, and is raised out of a state of imperfection and brought once more into perfect union with the Lord of life and glory into whose image he has thus become shaped and conformed.

It is in this large sense, then, that Masonry may become for us—as indeed it was intended to become by those who instituted our present speculative system—a working philosophy for those brought within its influence. It supplies a need to those who are earnestly enquiring into the purpose and destiny of human life. It is a means of initiating into reliable knowledge those who feel that their knowledge of life and their path of life have hitherto been but a series of irregular steps made at haphazard and under hoodwinked conditions as to whither they are going. Not without good reason does our catechism assert that Masonry contains " many and invaluable secrets." But these of course are not the formal and symbolic signs, tokens and words communicated ceremonially to candidates ; they are rather those secrets which we instinctively keep locked up in the recesses and safe repository of our hearts ; secrets of the deep and hidden things of the soul, about which we do not often talk, and which, by a natural instinct, we are not in the habit of communicating to any but such of our brethren and fellows as share with us a common and a sympathetic interest in the deeper problems and mysteries of life.

I have said already that Masonry is a modern perpetuation of great systems of initiation that have existed for the spiritual instruction of men in all parts of the world since the beginning of time. The reason for their existence has been the obvious one, resulting from the cardinal truth already alluded to, that man in his present natural state is inherently and radically imperfect; that sooner or later he becomes conscious of a sense of loss and deprivation and feels an imperative need of learning how to repair that loss. The great world-religions have been ordained to teach in their respective manners the same truths as the Mystery systems have taught. Their teaching has always been twofold. There has always existed an external, elementary, popular doctrine which has served for the instruction of the masses who are insufficiently prepared for deeper teaching; and concurrently therewith there has been an interior, advanced doctrine, a more secret knowledge, which has been reserved for riper minds and into which only proficient and properly prepared candidates, who voluntarily sought to participate in it, were initiated. Whether in ancient India, Egypt, Greece, Italy or Mexico, or among the Druids of Europe, temples of initiation have ever existed for those who felt the inward call to come apart from the multitude and to dedicate themselves to a long discipline of body and mind with a view to acquiring the secret knowledge and developing the spiritual faculties by means of experimental processes of initiation of which our present ceremonies are the faint echo. It is far

beyond my present scope to describe any of these
great systems or the methods of initiation they
employed. But in regard to them I will ask you
to accept my statement upon two points : (1) that
although these great schools of the Mysteries have
long dropped out of the public mind, they, or the
doctrine they taught, have never ceased to exist ;
the enmity of official ecclesiasticism and the tendencies of a materialistic and commercial age have
caused them to subside into extreme secrecy and
concealment, but their initiates have never been
absent from the world ; and (2) that it was through
the activity and foresight of some of these advanced
initiates that our present system of speculative
Masonry is due. You must not imply from this
that modern Masonry is by any means a full or
adequate presentation of these older and larger
systems. It is but their pale and elementary
shadow. But such as they are, and so far as they
do go, our rituals and doctrine are an authentic
embodiment of a secret doctrine and a secret
process that have always existed for the enlightenment of such aspirants as, putting their trust in
God (as our present candidates are made to say),
have knocked at the door of certain secret sanctuaries
in the confidence that that door would open and
that they would find in due course that for which
they were seeking. Those who instituted modern
speculative Masonry some 250 years ago took
certain materials lying ready to hand. They took,
that is, the elementary rites and symbols pertaining
to mediæval operative guilds of stone-masons and
transformed them into a system of religio-philosophic

doctrine. Thenceforward, from being related to the trade which deals in stones and bricks, the intention of Masonry was to deal solely and simply with the greater science of soul-building ; and, save for retaining certain analogies which the art of the practical stone-mason provided, thenceforward it became dedicated to purposes that are wholly spiritual, religious and philosophic.

Perhaps the chief evidence of the transformation thus effected was the incorporation of the central legend and traditional history comprised in our Third Degree. Obviously that legend can have had no relation to, or practical bearing upon, the operative builders' trade. I will ask you to reflect that no building of stone, no temple or other edifice capable of being built with hands, has remained unfinished through the death of any professional architect such as Hiram Abiff is popularly supposed to have been. The principles of architecture, the genuine secrets of the building trade, are not and never have been lost ; they are thoroughly well known, and the absurdity is manifest of supposing that Masons of any kind are waiting for time or circumstances to restore any lost knowledge as to the manner in which temporal buildings ought to be constructed. We know how to erect buildings to-day quite as well as our Hebrew forefathers did who built the famous temple at Jerusalem, and indeed a well-known architect has stated that most of our London churches are, both for size and ornamentation, far larger and more splendid than that temple ever was. Our duty then is to look behind the literal story ; to pierce the veil of allegory contained in the great legend and to grasp the significance of its true purport. That which is lost is to be found, we are told, with the Centre. But if we enquire what a Centre is, the average Mason will give you nothing more than the official, enigmatic and not very luminous answer that it is a point within a circle from which every part of the circumference is equidistant. But what circle? and what circumference?, for there are no such things as centres or circles in respect of ordinary buildings or architecture. And here the average Mason is at an utter loss to explain. Press him further, " Why with the Centre? " and again he can only give you the elusive and perplexing answer " Because that is a point from which a Master Mason cannot err," and you are no wiser.

Brethren, it is just this elusiveness, these intentional enigmas, this purposed puzzle-language, that are intended to put us on the scent of something deeper than the words themselves convey, and if we fail to find, to realize and to act upon, the intention of what is veiled behind the letter of the rituals, we can scarcely claim to understand our own doctrine; we can scarcely claim to have been regularly initiated, passed and raised in the higher sense of those expressions, whatever ceremonies we have formally passed through. " The letter killeth, the spirit giveth life." Let us enquire what the spirit of this puzzle-language is.

The method of all great religious and initiatory systems has been to teach their doctrine in the form of myth, legend or allegory. As our first tracing-board lecture says, " The philosophers,

67

unwilling to expose their mysteries to vulgar eyes, concealed their tenets and principles of philosophy under hieroglyphical figures," and our traditional history is one of these hieroglyphical figures. Now the literally-minded never see behind the letter of the allegory. The truly initiated mind discerns the allegory's spiritual value. In fact, part of the purpose of all initiation was, and still is, to educate the mind in penetrating the outward shell of all phenomena, and the value of initiation depends upon the way in which the inward truths are allowed to influence our thought and lives and to awaken in us still deeper powers of consciousness.

The legend of the Third Degree, then, in which the essence of Masonic doctrine lies, was brought into our system by some advanced minds who derived their knowledge from other and concealed sources. The legend is an adaptation of a very old one and existed in various forms long before its association with modern Masonry. In the guise of a story about the building of a temple by King Solomon at Jerusalem, they were promulgating the truth which I have alluded to before and which is generally known as the Fall of Man. As our legend runs, upon the literal side of it, it was the purpose of a great king to erect a superb structure. He was assisted in that work by another king who supplied the building materials, by a skilful artificer whose business was to put these together according to a pre-ordained plan, and by large companies of craftsmen and labourers. But in the course of the work an evil conspiracy arose, resulting in the destruction of the chief artificer and preventing the completion of the building, which remains unfinished, therefore, to this day.

Now I will ask you to observe that this legend cannot refer to any historical building built in the old metropolis of Palestine. If we refer to the Bible as an authority you will find that that temple *was* completed ; it was afterwards destroyed, rebuilt and destroyed again on more than one occasion. Moreover, the biblical accounts make no reference whatever to the conspiracy, or to the death of Hiram. On the other hand they state expressly that Hiram " made an end of building " the temple ; that it was finished and completed in every particular. It is very clear then that we must keep the two subjects entirely separate in our minds ; and recognize that the Masonic story deals with something quite distinct from the biblical story. What temple then is referred to ? The temple, brethren, that is still incomplete and unfinished is none that can be built with hands. It is that temple of which all material edifices are but the types and symbols : it is the temple of the collective body of humanity itself ; of which the great initiate St. Paul said " Know ye not that *ye* are the temple of God ? " A perfect humanity was the great Temple which, in the counsels of the Most High, was intended to be reared in the mystical Holy City, of which the local Jerusalem was the type. The three great Master-builders, Solomon and the two Hirams, are a triad corresponding after a manner with the Holy Trinity of the Christian religion ; Hiram Abiff being the chief architect, he " by whom all things were made " and " in whom (as St. Paul said, using

69

Masonic language) the whole building fitly framed together groweth unto a holy temple in the Lord." The material of this mystical temple was the souls of men, at once the living stones, the fellow craftsmen and collaborators with the divine purpose.

But in the course of the construction of this ideal temple, something happened that wrecked the scheme and delayed the fulfilment indefinitely. This was the Fall of Man; the conspiracy of the craftsmen. Turn to the book of Genesis, you will find the same subject related in the allegory of Adam and Eve. They were intended, as you know, for perfection and happiness, but their Creator's project became nullified by their disobedience to certain conditions imposed upon them. I will ask you to observe that their offence was precisely that committed by our Masonic conspirators. They had been forbidden to eat of the Tree of Knowledge; or, in Masonic language, they were under obligation " not to attempt to extort the secrets of a superior degree " which they had not attained. Now the Hebrew word Hiram means *Guru*, teacher of " supreme knowledge," divine light and wisdom, and the liberty that comes therewith. But this knowledge is only for the perfected man. It is that knowledge that Hiram said was " known to but three in the world," *i.e.*, known only in the counsels of the Divine Trinity, but it is knowledge that with patience and perseverance every Mason, every child of the Creator, " may in due time become entitled to a participation in." But just as Adam and Eve's attempt to obtain illicit knowledge caused their expulsion from Eden and defeated the divine purpose until they and their posterity should regain the Paradise they had lost, so also the completion of the great mystical Temple was prevented for the time being by the conspirators' attempt to extort from Hiram the Master's secrets, and its construction is delayed until time and circumstances—God's time, and the circumstances we create for ourselves—restore to us the lost and genuine secrets of our nature and of the divine purpose in us.

The tragedy of Hiram Abiff, then, is not the record of any vulgar, brutal murder of an individual man. It is a parable of cosmic and universal loss ; an allegory of the breakdown of a divine scheme. We are dealing with no calamity that occurred during the erection of a building in an eastern city, but with a moral disaster to universal humanity. Hiram is slain ; in other words, the faculty of enlightened wisdom has been cut off from us. Owing to that disaster mankind is here to-day in this world of imperfect knowledge, of limited faculties, of chequered happiness, of perpetual toil, of death and frequent bitterness and pain ; our life here is (to use a poet's words) :—

" An ever-moaning battle in the mist,
   Death in all life and lying in all love ;
   The meanest having power upon the highest,
   And the high purpose broken by the worm."

The temple of human nature is unfinished and we know not how to complete it. The want of plans and designs to regulate the disorders of individual and social life indicates to us all that some heavy calamity has befallen us as a race. The absence of a clear and guiding principle in the world's life reminds us of the utter confusion into which the absence of that Supreme Wisdom, which is personified as Hiram, has thrown us all, and causes every reflective mind to attribute to some fatal catastrophe his mysterious disappearance. We all long for that light and wisdom which have become lost to us. Like the craftsmen in search of the body, we go our different ways in search of what is lost. Many of us make no discovery of importance throughout the length of our days. We seek it in pleasure, in work, in all the varied occupations and diversions of our lives; we seek it in intellectual pursuits, in religion, in Masonry, and those who search farthest and deepest are those who become most conscious of the loss and who are compelled to cry " Machabone ! Macbenah ! the Master is smitten," or, as the Christian Scriptures word it, " They have taken away my Lord, and I know not where they have laid him."

Hiram Abiff is slain. The high light and wisdom ordained to guide and enlighten humanity are wanting to us. The full blaze of light and perfect knowledge that were to be ours are vanished from the race, but in the Divine Providence there still remains to us a glimmering light in the East. In a dark world, from which as it were the sun has disappeared, we have still our five senses and our rational faculties to work with, and these provide us with the substituted secrets that must distinguish us before we regain the genuine ones.

Where is Hiram buried ? We are taught that the Wisdom of the Most High—personified as King

Solomon—ordered him to be interred in a fitting sepulchre outside the Holy City, " in a grave from the centre 3 feet between N. and S., 3 feet between E. and W., and 5 feet or more perpendicular." Where, Brethren, do you imagine that grave to be ? Can you locate it by following these minute details of its situation ? Probably you have never thought of the matter as other than an ordinary burial outside the walls of a geographical Jerusalem. But the grave of Hiram is *ourselves*. Each of us is the sepulchre in which the smitten Master is interred. If we know it not it is a further sign of our benighted-ness. At the centre of ourselves, deeper than any dissecting-knife can reach or than any physical investigation can fathom, lies buried the " vital and immortal principle," the " glimmering ray " that affiliates us to the Divine Centre of all life, and that is never wholly extinguished however evil or imperfect our lives may be. *We* are the grave of the Master. The lost guiding light is buried at the centre of ourselves. High as your hand may reach upwards or downwards from the centre of your own body—*i.e.*, 3 feet between N. and S.— far as it can reach to right or left of the middle of your person—*i.e.*, 3 feet between W. and E.—and 5 feet or more perpendicular—the height of the human body—these are the indications by which our cryptic ritual describes the tomb of Hiram Abiff at the centre of ourselves. He is buried " outside the Holy City," in the same sense that the posterity of Adam have all been placed outside the walls of Paradise, for, " nothing unclean can enter into the holy place " which elsewhere in our Scriptures is called the Kingdom of Heaven.

What then is this " Centre," by reviving and using which we may hope to regain the secrets of our lost nature ? We may reason from analogies. As the Divine Life and Will is the centre of the whole universe and controls it ; as the sun is the centre and life-giver of our solar system and controls and feeds with life the planets circling round it, so at the secret centre of individual human life exists a vital, immortal principle, the spirit and the spiritual will of man. This is the faculty, by using which (when we have found it) we can never err. It is a point within the circle of our own nature and, living as we do in this physical world, the circle of our existence is bounded by two grand parallel lines ; " one representing Moses ; the other King Solomon," that is to say, law and wisdom ; the divine ordinances regulating the universe on the one hand ; the divine " wisdom and mercy that follow us all the days of our life " on the other. Very truly then the Mason who keeps himself thus circumscribed cannot err.

Masonry, then, is a system of religious philosophy in that it provides us with a doctrine of the universe and of our place in it. It indicates whence we are come and whither we may return. It has two purposes. Its first purpose is to show that man has fallen away from a high and holy centre to the circumference or externalized condition in which we now live ; to indicate that those who so desire may regain that centre by finding the centre in ourselves, for, since Deity is as a circle whose centre is every-

where, it follows that a divine centre, a " vital and
immortal principle," exists within ourselves by
developing which we may hope to regain our lost
and primal stature. The second purpose of the
Craft doctrine is to declare the way by which that
centre may be found within ourselves, and this
teaching is embodied in the discipline and ordeals
delineated in the three degrees. The Masonic
doctrine of the Centre—or, in other words, the
Christian axiom that " the Kingdom of Heaven is
within you "—is nowhere better stated than by the
poet Browning :

> " Truth is within ourselves. It takes no rise
> From outward things, whate'er you may believe.
> There is an inmost centre in ourselves
> Where truth abides in fullness ; and to know
> Rather consists in finding out a way
> Whence the imprisoned splendour may escape
> Than by effecting entrance for a light
> Supposed to be without."

Brethren, may we all come to the knowledge how
to " open the Lodge upon the centre " of ourselves
and so realize in our own conscious experience the
finding of the " imprisoned splendour " hidden in
the depths of our being, whose rising within ourselves will bring us peace and salvation. How then
does the Craft doctrine prescribe for the liberation
of this imprisoned centre ? Its first injunctions are
those of our first degree. There must be purity of
thought and purpose. I need scarcely remind you
that the word candidate derives from the Latin
candidus, white (in the sense of purity), or that our
postulants before entering the Lodge leave behind
them in the precincts the garments that belong to

the fashion of the outer world whose ideals they are desirous of relinquishing, and enter the Lodge clad in white as emblematic of the blamelessness of their thought and the purification of their lives. As this symbolic white clothing is worn during each of the three degrees, it is as though the seeker after the high light of the Centre must always come uttering the triple ascription, " Holy, Holy, Holy," as the token of the threefold purity of body, soul and spirit, which is essential to the achievement of his quest. He has left all money and metals behind him, for the gross things of this world are superfluous in the world that lies within ; whilst if any dross of thought or imperfections of character remain in him, he will find the impossibility of attaining to the consciousness of his highest self ; he will learn that he must renounce them and begin again, and that his attempt at real initiation must be repeated.

He must be animated by a spirit of universal sympathy. Financial doles and practical relief to the pecuniarily poor and distressed are admirable practices as far as they go, but they by no means exhaust the meaning of the term charity as Masonry intends it. The payment of a few guineas to philanthropic institutions is scarcely a fulfilment of St. Paul's great definition of charity so often read in our Lodges, by exercising which we are wont to say that a Mason " attains the summit of his profession."

There is a far larger sense of Brotherhood than the limited conventional one obtaining among those who are members of a common association. There is that deep sense in which a man feels himself not only in fraternity with his fellow-men, whether masonically his brethren or not, but realizes himself brother to all that is, part of the universal life that thrills through all things. A great illuminate, St. Francis of Assisi, expressed what I refer to when he wrote in his famous canticle, of his brothers the sun and the wind; his sisters the moon and the sea; his brethren the animals and the birds; as being all parts of a common life, all constituents in the scheme of the Great Architect for the restoration of the Temple of Creation and its dedication to His service, and as all worthy of a common love upon our part, even as they are the subject of a common solicitude upon His.

And passing from these primary qualifications we proceed to what is signified by our second degree, wherein is inculcated the analysis and cultivation of the mental and rational faculties; the study of the secrets of the marvellous, complex, psychical nature of man; the relation of these with the still higher and spiritual part of him which, in turn, he may learn to trace " even to the throne of God Himself " with which he is affiliated at the root essence of his being. These studies, brethren, so lightly touched upon in our passing-ceremony, so glibly referred to as we recite our ritual, when undertaken with the seriousness that attached to them in the old mystery-systems are not without just reason described in our own words as " serious, solemn and awful." The depths of human nature and self-knowledge, the hidden mysteries of the soul of man are not, as real initiates well know, probed into with impunity except by the " properly prepared." The man who does so has, as it were, a cable-tow around his neck; because when once stirred by a genuine desire for the higher knowledge that real initiation is intended to confer, he can never turn back on what he learns thereof without committing moral suicide; he can never be again the same man he was before he gained a glimpse of the hidden mysteries of life. And as the Angel stood with a flaming sword at the entrance of Eden to guard the way to the Tree of Life, so will the man whose initiation is not a conventional one find himself threatened at the door of the higher knowledge by opposing invisible forces if he rashly rushes forward in a state of moral unfitness into the deep secrets of the Centre. Better remain ignorant than embark upon this unknown sea unwisely and without being properly prepared and in possession of the proper passports.

And eventually the aspirant, after these preliminary disciplines, has to learn the great truth embodied in the third degree; that he who would be raised to perfection and regain what he has long realized has been lost to himself, may do so only by utter self-abnegation, by a dying to all that to the eyes and the reason of the uninitiated outer world is precious and desirable. The third degree, brethren, is an exposition in dramatic ceremonial of the text "Whoso would save his life must lose it." Beneath the allegory of the death of the Master— and remember that it *is* allegory—is expressed the universal truth that mystical death must precede mystical rebirth. " Know ye not that ye must be born again ? " " Unless a grain of corn fall into the ground and die, it abideth alone; if it die it bringeth forth much fruit." And it is only thus that all Master-Masons can be raised from a figurative (not a physical) death to a regenerated state and to the full stature of human nature.

The path of true initiation into fullness of life by way of a figurative death to one's lower self is the path called in the Scriptures the narrow way, of which it is also said that few there be who find it. It is the narrow path between the Pillars, for Boaz and Jachin stand impliedly at the entrance of every Masonic Temple and between them we pass each time we enter the Lodge. Very great prominence is accorded these pillars in the ritual, but very little explanation of their import is given, and it is desirable to know something of their great significance. To deal with them at all fully would require an entire lecture upon this one subject, and even then there would have to remain unsaid in regard to these great symbols much that is unsuited to treatment in a general lecture.

The pillars form, and have always formed, a prominent feature in the temples of all great systems of religion and initiation, whether Masonic or not. They have been incorporated into Christian architecture. If you recall the construction of York Minster or Westminster Abbey, you will recognize the pillars in the two great towers flanking the main entrance to those cathedrals at the west end of the structure. Non-Masons, therefore, enter these temples, as we do, between the pillars in the West; they look through them along the straight path that leads to the high altar, just as the Mason's symbolic passage is also from the West to the throne in the

East. That path is, as it were, the straight path of life, beginning in this outer world and terminating at the throne, or altar, in the East. Many centuries before our Bible was written or the temple of Solomon described in the Books of Kings and Chronicles was thought of, the two pillars were used in the great temples of the Mysteries in Egypt, and one of the great annual public festivals was that of the setting up of the pillars. What, then, did they signify ? I can deal with the subject but very superficially here. In one of their aspects they stand for what is known in Eastern philosophy as the " pairs of opposites." Everything in nature is dual and can only be known in contrast with its opposite, whilst the two in combination produce a metaphysical third which is their synthesis and perfect balance. Thus we have good and evil ; light and darkness (and one of the pillars was always white and the other black) ; active and passive ; positive and negative ; yes and no ; outside and inside ; man and woman. Neither of these is complete without the other ; taken together they form stability. Morning and evening unite to form the complete day. Man is proverbially imperfect without his " better half," woman ; the two marry to impart strength to each other and to establish their common house. Physical science shows all matter to be composed of positive and negative electric forces in perfect balance and that things would disintegrate and disappear if they did not stand firm in perfect union. Every drop of healthy blood in our bodies is a combination of red and white corpuscles, by the due balance of

which we are established in strength and health, *Masonry*
whilst lack of balance is attended by disease. The *as a*
pillars therefore typify, in one of their aspects, *Philo-*
perfect integrity of body and soul such as are *sophy*
essential to achieving spiritual perfection. In the
terms of ancient philosophy all created things are
composed of fire and water ; fire being their spiritual
and water their material element, and so the pillars
represented also these universal properties. In one
of the Apocryphal Scriptures (2 Esdras, 7 ; 7-8), the
path to true wisdom and life is spoken of as an
entrance between a fire on the right hand and a
deep water on the left, and so narrow and painful
that only one man may go through it at once. This
is in allusion to the narrow and painful path of real
initiation of which our entrance into the Lodge
between the pillars is a symbol.

Now all great symbols are shadowed forth in the
person of man himself. The human organism is
the true Lodge that must be opened and wherein
the great Mysteries are to be found, and our Lodge-
rooms are so built and furnished as to typify the
human organism. The lower and physical part of
us is animal and earthy, and rests, like the base of
Jacob's ladder, upon the earth ; whilst our higher
portion is spiritual and reaches to the heavens.
These two portions of ourselves are in perpetual con-
flict, the spiritual and the carnal ever warring against
one another ; and he alone is the wise man who has
learned to effect a perfect balance between them and
to establish himself in strength so that his own inward
house stands firm against all weakness and tempta-
tion. And in still another sense the two pillars may

be seen exemplified in the human body. There are our two legs, upon both of which we must stand firm to acquire a perfect physical balance. And having discerned this simple truth, and having seen that the path of true initiation, which is one of spiritual rebirth, is an arduous and painful progress to him who undertakes it, let me ask you to consider in all sacredness another physical phenomenon, the great mystery of which we perhaps think little of by reason of its frequency and of our familiarity with it. I refer to the incident—the great mystery, I might say—of child-birth. Brethren, every child born into this world, coming into this life as into a great house of initiation, trial and discipline, passes, amid pain and travail, through a strait and narrow way and between the two pillars that support the temple of its mother's body. And thus in the commonplaces of life, in which for those who have clean hearts there is nothing common or unclean but everything is sacred and symbolic, the act of physical birth is an image and a foreshadowing of that mystical rebirth and of that passing through a strait gate and a narrow way in a deeper sense, without which it is written that a man shall not enter into the Kingdom of Heaven.

The regenerated man, the man who not merely in ceremonial form but in vital experience, has passed through the phases of which the Masonic degrees are the faint symbol, is alone worthy of the title of Master-Mason in the building of the Temple that is not made with hands but that is being built invisibly out of the souls of just men made perfect. Not only in this world is this temple being built;

only the foundations of the intended structure are perceptible here. The Craft contemplates other and loftier planes of life, other storeys of the vast structure than this we live and work in. Just as our Craft organization has its higher assemblies and councils in the form of the Provincial and the Grand Lodges that regulate and minister to the need of the Lodges of common craftsmen, so in the mighty system of the universal structure there are grades of higher life, hierarchies of celestial beings working and ministering in the loftier portions of the building, beyond our present ken. And as here at the head of our limited and temporal brotherhood there rules a Grand Master, so too over the cosmic system there presides the Great Architect and Most Worshipful Grand Master of all, whose officers are holy Angels; and the recognition of this truth may tend to consecrate us in the discharge of the little symbolic part we severally perform in the system which is the image of the great scheme.

The world at large, Brethren, is as it were, but one great Lodge and place of initiation, of which our Masonic Lodges are the little mirrors. Mother-Earth is also the Mother-Lodge of us all. As its vast work goes on, souls are ever descending into it and souls are being called out of it at the knocks of some great unseen Warden of life and death, who calls them here to labour and summons them hence for refreshment. After the Lodge, the festive board; after the labour of this world, the repast and refreshment of the heavenly places. And thus, although our after-proceedings have no formal place in the Masonic system, any more than the after-life is in formal connection with us whilst our sphere of activity is in this present world, still it plays a striking and appropriate part calculated to awaken us to the deep significance of our customary conviviality. Upon such occasions we are wont to drink the toast of " the King and the Craft," remembering as loyal subjects and loving brethren our earthly sovereign and our Masonic comrades throughout the world. But here again I would ask every Master who gives and every brother who drinks this toast, to lift his thoughts to a greater King and to a larger craft than our limited and symbolic fraternity. I would remind you how in the Christian Mysteries there was another Master whom unconsciously we imitate, who also after supper took the cup and when he had given thanks to the King of kings, pledged himself, as it were, to that larger Craft which is co-extensive with humanity itself; directing them in this manner to show forth symbolically a certain great mystery until his coming again. But this, Brethren, is none other than what is implied in our own Masonic words when we also are directed to use certain substituted secrets until time and circumstances shall restore to us the genuine ones.

In submitting, then, these thoughts to you, it may be claimed that Masonry offers to those capable of appreciating it a working philosophy and a practical rule of life. It discloses to us the scheme of the universe—a scheme once shattered and arrested, but left in the hands of humanity to restore. It indicates our place, our purpose and our destiny in that universe. It is as a great house of instruction and initiation into the Mysteries of a larger and fuller life than the unenlightened worldling is as yet ripe for appreciating. Let us, therefore, value and endeavour fully to appreciate its mysteries. Let us also be careful not to cheapen the Order by failing to realize its meaning and by admitting to its ranks those who are unready or unfitted to understand its import. I said at the outset of this lecture that some Masons are beginning to awake to a larger consciousness of the true meaning and purport of our Craft. I say now at the end, Brethren! lift up your hearts; throw wide open the shutters of your minds and imaginations. Learn to see in Masonry something more than a parochial system enjoining elementary morality, performing perfunctory and meaningless rites, and serving as an agreeable accessory to social life. But look to find in it a living philosophy, a vital guide upon those matters which of all others are the most sacred and the most urgent to our ultimate well-being. Realize that its secrets which are " many and invaluable " are not upon the surface ; that they are not those of the tongue, but of the heart ; and that its mysteries are those eternal ones that treat of the spirit rather than of the body of man. And with this knowledge clothe yourselves and enter the Lodge—not merely the Lodge-room of our symbolic Craft, but the larger Lodge of life, wherein, silently and without the sound of metal tool, is proceeding the perpetual work of rebuilding the unfinished and invisible Temple of which the mystical stones and timber are the souls of men. In that rebuilding, men and women are taking part who, whilst formally not members of our Craft, are still unconsciously Masons in the best of senses. For whosoever is carefully and deliberately " squaring his stone " is fitting himself for his place in the " intended structure " which gradually is being " put together with exact nicety " and which, though erected by ourselves, one day will become manifest to our clearer vision and will appear " more like the work of the Great Architect of the Universe than that of human hands."   Upon us Masons therefore, who have the advantage of a regular and organized system which provides and inculcates for us an outline of the great truths that we have been considering and that always in the world have been regarded as secret, as sacred, and as vital, there rests the responsibility attaching to our privilege, and it must be our aim to endeavour to enter into the full heritage of understanding and practising the system to which we belong.

Chapter III

FURTHER NOTES ON CRAFT SYMBOLISM.

" There is no darkness but ignorance." (*Shakespeare*).

" Lighten our darkness, we beseech Thee, and defend
us from all perils and dangers of this night."

(Anglican Liturgy).

" Belov'd All-Father, and all you gods that haunt this
place, grant me to be beautiful in the inner man, and
all I have of outer things to be one with those within !
May I count only the wise man rich, and may my
store of gold be such as none but the good can bear.
Anything more ? That prayer, I think, is enough
for me ! " (*Prayer of Socrates*).

IN the Lecture on the First Degree tracing-
board Masonry is spoken of as " an art founded
on the principles of Geometry," and also as
being " a science dealing with the cultivation and
improvement of the human mind." Its usages and
customs are also there said to have derived " from
the ancient Egyptians whose philosophers, unwilling
to expose their mysteries to vulgar eyes, conceal their
principles and philosophy under signs and symbols,"
which are still perpetuated in the Masonic Order.

Something of these signs and symbols, as well as
the purpose of the Masonic system as a whole,
has already been outlined in previous papers. In
the present notes it is proposed to extend the
consideration of the subject in greater detail.

The Instruction Lectures associated with each
Degree of the Craft purport to expound the doctrine
of the system and interpret the symbols and rituals.
But these Lectures themselves stand in similar need

of interpretation. Indeed, they are contrived with very great cunning and concealment. Their compilers were confronted with the dual task of giving a faithful, if partial, expression of esoteric doctrine and at the same time of so masking it that its full sense would not be understood without some effort or enlightenment, and should convey little or nothing at all to those unworthy of or unripe for the " gnosis " or wisdom-teaching. They discharged that task with signal success and in a way which provokes admiration from those who can appreciate it for their profound knowledge of, and insight into, the science of self-knowledge and regeneration. They were obviously Initiates of an advanced type, well versed in the secret tradition and philosophy of the Mystery systems of the past and acutely perceptive of the deeper and mystical sense of the Holy Scriptures to which they constantly make luminous reference.

To deal with these explanatory Lectures in complete detail would involve a very long task. We will, however, proceed to speak of some of the more prominent matters with which they deal and so elaborate the subject-matter of our previous papers.

Attention must first be called to the term " Geometry," the art upon which the entire system is stated to be founded. To the ordinary man Geometry means nothing more than the branch of mathematics associated with the problems of Euclid, a subject obviously having no relation to Masonic ceremonial and ideals. Another explanation of the term must therefore be looked for.

Now Geometry was one of the " seven noble arts

and sciences " of ancient philosophy. It means literally the science of earth-measurement. But the " earth " of the ancients did not mean, as it does to us, this physical planet. It meant the primordial substance, or undifferentiated soul-stuff out of which we human beings have been created, the " mother-earth " from which we have all sprung and to which we must all undoubtedly return. Man was made, the Scriptures teach, out of the dust of the ground, and it is that ground, that earth or fundamental substance of his being, which requires to be " measured " in the sense of investigating and understanding its nature and properties. No competent builder erects a structure without first satisfying himself about the nature of the materials with which he proposes to build, and in the speculative or spiritual and " royal " art of Masonry no Mason can properly build the temple of his own soul without first understanding the nature of the raw material he has to work upon.

Geometry, therefore, is synonymous with self-knowledge, the understanding of the basic substance of our being, its properties and potentialities. Over the ancient temples of initiation was inscribed the sentence " Know thyself and thou shalt know the universe and God," a phrase which implies in the first place that the uninitiated man is without knowledge of himself, and in the second place that when he attains that knowledge he will realize himself to be no longer the separate distinctified individual he now supposes himself to be, but to be a microcosm or summary of all that is and to be identified with the Being of God.

Masonry is the science of the attainment of that supreme knowledge and is, therefore, rightly said to be founded on the principles of Geometry as thus defined.

But do not let it be supposed that the physical matter of which our mortal bodies are composed is the " earth " referred to. That is but corruptible impermanent stuff which merely forms a temporary encasement of the imperishable true " earth " or substance of our souls, and enables them to enter into sense-relations with the physical world. The distinction must be clearly grasped and held in mind, for Masonry has to deal not so much with the transient outward body as with the eternal inward being of man, although the outward body is temporarily involved with the latter. It is the immortal soul of man which is the ruined temple and needs to be rebuilt upon the principles of spiritual science. The mortal body of it, with its unruly wills and affections, stands in the way of that achievement. It is the rubble which needs to be cleared before the new foundations can be set and the new structure reared. Yet even rubble can be made to serve useful purposes and be rearranged and worked into the new erection, and accordingly man's outer temporal nature can be disciplined and utilized in the reconstruction of himself. But in order to effect this reconstruction he must first have a full understanding of the material he has to work with and to work upon. For this purpose he must be made acquainted with what is called " the form of the Lodge."

THE FORM OF THE LODGE

This is officially described as " an oblong square ; in length between East and West, in breadth between North and South, in depth from the surface of the earth to its centre, and even as high as the heavens."

This is interpretable as alluding to the human individual. Man himself is a Lodge. And just as the Masonic Lodge is " an assemblage of brethren and fellows met to expatiate upon the mysteries of the Craft," so individual man is a composite being made up of various properties and faculties assembled together in him with a view to their harmonious interaction and working out the purpose of life. It must always be remembered that everything in Masonry is figurative of *man* and his human constitution and spiritual evolution. Accordingly, the Masonic Lodge is sacramental of the individual Mason as he is when he seeks admission to a Lodge. A man's first entry into a Lodge is symbolical of his first entry upon the science of knowing himself.

His organism is symbolised by a four-square or four-sided building. This is in accordance with the very ancient philosophical doctrine that four is the arithmetical symbol of everything which has manifested or physical form. Spirit, which is unmanifest and not physical, is expressed by the number three and the triangle. But Spirit which has so far projected itself as to become objective and wear a material form or body, is denoted by the number four and the quadrangle or square. Hence the Hebrew name of Deity, as known and worshipped in this outer world, was the great

91

unspeakable name of four letters or Tetragrammaton, whilst the cardinal points of space are also four, and every manifested thing is a compound of the four basic metaphysical elements called by the ancients fire, water, air and earth. The four-sidedness of the Lodge, therefore, is also a reminder that the human organism is compounded of those four elements in balanced proportions. " Water " represents the psychic nature ; "Air," the mentality ; " Fire," the will and nervous force ; whilst " Earth " is the condensation in which the other three become stabilized and encased.

But it is an oblongated (or duplicated) square, because man's organism does not consist of his physical body alone. The physical body has its " double " or ethereal counterpart in the astral body, which is an extension of the physical nature and a compound of the same four elements in an im-palpable and more tenuous form. The oblong spatial form of the Lodge must therefore be considered as referable to the physical and ethereal nature of man in the conjunction in which they in fact consist in each of us.

The four sides of the Lodge have a further significance. The East of the Lodge represents man's spirituality, his highest and most spiritual mode of consciousness, which in most men is very little developed, if at all, but is still latent and slumbering and becomes active only in moments of stress or deep emotion. The West (or polar opposite of the East) represents his normal rational under-standing, the consciousness he employs in temporal every-day affairs, his material-mindedness or, as we

might say, his " common sense."   Midway between
these East and West extremes is the South, the
halfway house and meeting-place of the spiritual
intuition and the rational understanding ; the point
denoting abstract intellectuality and our intellectual
power develops to its highest, just as the sun attains
its meridian splendour in the South.   The antipodes
of this is the North, the sphere of benightedness
and ignorance, referable to merely sense-reactions
and impressions received by that lowest and least
reliable mode of perception, our physical sense-
nature.

Thus the four sides of the Lodge point to four
different, yet progressive, modes of consciousness
available to us.   Sense-impression (North), reason
(West), intellectual ideation (South), and spiritual
intuition (East) ; making up our four possible ways
of knowledge.   Of these the ordinary man employs
only the first two or perhaps three, in accordance
with his development and education, and his outlook on life and knowledge of truth are correspondingly restricted and imperfect.   Full and
perfect knowledge is possible only when the deep-
seeing vision and consciousness of man's spiritual
principle have been awakened and superadded to
his other cognitive faculties.   This is possible only
to the true Master, who has all four methods of
knowledge at his disposal in perfect balance and
adjusted like the four sides of the Lodge ; and
hence the place of the Master and Past-Masters
being always in the East.

The " depth " of the Lodge (" from the surface
of the earth to its centre ") refers to the distance or

difference of degree between the superficial consciousness of our earthly mentality and the supreme
divine degree of consciousness resident at man's
spiritual centre when he has become able to open
his Lodge upon that centre and to function in and
with it.

The " height " of the Lodge (" even as high as
the heavens ") implies that the range of consciousness possible to us, when we have developed our
potentialities to the full, is infinite.   Man who has
sprung from the earth and developed through the
lower kingdoms of nature to his present rational
state, has yet to complete his evolution by becoming
a god-like being and unifying his consciousness with
the Omniscient—to promote which is and always
has been the sole aim and purpose of all Initiation.

To scale this " height," to attain this expansion
of consciousness, is achieved " by the use of a
ladder of many rounds or staves, but of three
principal ones, Faith, Hope and Charity," of which
the greatest and most effectual is the last.   That is
to say, there are innumerable ways of developing
one's consciousness to higher degrees, and in fact
every common-place incident of daily experience
may contribute to that end if it be rightly interpreted
and its purpose in the general pattern of our life-
scheme be discerned ; yet even these should be
subordinate to the three chief qualifications, namely,
Faith in the possibility of attaining the end in view ;
Hope, or a persistent fervent desire for its fulfilment ; and finally an unbounded Love which,
seeking God in all men and all things, despite their
outward appearances, and thinking no evil, gradually

identifies the mind and nature of the aspirant with that ultimate Good upon which his thought, desire and gaze should be persistently directed.

It is important to note here that this enlargement of consciousness is in no way represented as being dependent upon intellectual attainments, learning or book-knowledge. These may be, and indeed are, lesser staves of the ladder of attainment; but they are not numbered among the principal ones. Compare St. Paul's words " Though I have all knowledge and have not love, I am nothing;" and those of a mediæval mystic " By love He may be gotten and holden, but by wit and understanding never."

The Lodge is " supported by three grand pillars, Wisdom, Strength and Beauty." Again the references are not to the external meeting-place, but to a triplicity of properties resident in the individual soul, which will become increasingly manifest in the aspirant as he progresses and adapts himself to the Masonic discipline. As is written of the youthful Christian Master that " he increased in wisdom and stature and in favour with God and man," so will it also become true of the neophyte Mason who aspires to Mastership. He will become conscious of an increase of perceptive faculty and understanding; he will become aware of having tapped a previously unsuspected source of power, giving him enhanced mental strength and self-confidence; there will become observable in him developing graces of character, speech and conduct that were previously foreign to him.

The Floor, or groundwork of the Lodge, a

95

chequer-work of black and white squares, denotes the dual quality of everything connected with terrestrial life and the physical groundwork of human nature—the mortal body and its appetites and affections. " The web of our life is a mingled yarn, good and ill together," wrote Shakespeare. Everything material is characterized by inextricably interblended good and evil, light and shade, joy and sorrow, positive and negative. What is good for me may be evil for you; pleasure is generated from pain and ultimately degenerates into pain again; what it is right to do at one moment may be wrong the next; I am intellectually exalted to-day and to-morrow correspondingly depressed and benighted. The dualism of these opposites governs us in everything, and experience of it is prescribed for us until such time as, having learned and outgrown its lesson, we are ready for advancement to a condition where we outgrow the sense of this chequer-work existence and those opposites cease to be perceived as opposites, but are realized as a unity or synthesis. To find that unity or synthesis is to know the peace which passes understanding—*i.e.* which surpasses our present experience, because in it the darkness and the light are both alike, and our present concepts of good and evil, joy and pain, are transcended and found sublimated in a condition combining both. And this lofty condition is represented by the indented or tesselated border skirting the black and white chequer-work, even as the Divine Presence and Providence surrounds and embraces our temporal organisms in which those opposites are inherent.

Why is the chequer floor-work given such prominence in the Lodge-furniture? The answer is to be found in the statement in the Third Degree Ritual : " The square pavement is for the High Priest to walk upon." Now it is not merely the Jewish High Priest of centuries ago that is here referred to, but the individual member of the Craft. For every Mason is intended to be the High Priest of his own personal temple and to make of it a place where he and Deity may meet. By the mere fact of being in this dualistic world every living being, whether a Mason or not, walks upon the square pavement of mingled good and evil in every action of his life, so that the floor-cloth is the symbol of an elementary philosophical truth common to us all. But, for us, the words "walk upon" imply much more than that. They mean that he who aspires to be master of his fate and captain of his soul must walk upon these opposites in the sense of transcending and dominating them, of trampling upon his lower sensual nature and keeping it beneath his feet in subjection and control. He must become able to rise above the motley of good and evil, to be superior and indifferent to the ups and downs of fortune, the attractions and fears governing ordinary men and swaying their thoughts and actions this way or that. His object is the development of his innate spiritual potencies, and it is impossible that these should develop so long as he is over-ruled by his material tendencies and the fluctuating emotions of pleasure and pain that they give birth to. It is by rising superior to these and attaining serenity and mental equilibrium. under any circumstances in

which for the moment he may be placed, that a
Mason truly " walks upon " the chequered groundwork of existence and the conflicting tendencies of
his more material nature.

The Covering of the Lodge is shown in sharp
contrast to its black and white flooring and is
described as " a celestial canopy of divers colours,
even the heavens."

If the flooring symbolizes man's earthy sensuous
nature, the ceiling typifies his ethereal nature, his
" heavens " and the properties resident therein.
The one is the reverse and the opposite pole of the
other. His material body is visible and densely
composed. His ethereal surround, or " aura," is
tenuous and invisible, (save to clairvoyant vision),
and like the fragrance thrown off by a flower.
Its existence will be doubted by those unprepared
to accept what is not physically demonstrable, but
the Masonic student, who will be called upon to
accept many such truths provisionally until he knows
them as certainties, should reflect (1) that he
has entered the Craft with the professed object of
receiving light upon the nature of his own being,
(2) that the Order engages to assist him to that
light in regard to matters of which he is
admittedly ignorant, and that its teachings and
symbols were devised by wise and competent
instructors in such matters, and (3) that a humble,
docile and receptive mental attitude towards those
symbols and their meanings will better conduce to
his advancement than a critical or hostile one.

The fact that man throws off, or radiates from himself, an ethereal surround or " covering " is testified to by the aureoles and haloes shown in works of art about the persons of saintly characters. The unsaintly are not so distinctified, not because they are not so surrounded, but because in their case the " aura " exists as but an irregularly shaped and coloured cloud reflecting their normal undisciplined mentality and passional nature, as the rain-clouds reflect the sunlight in different tints. The " aura " of the man who has his mentality clean and his passions and emotions well in hand becomes a correspondingly orderly and shapely encasement of clearly defined form and iridescence, regularly striated like the colours of the spectrum or the rainbow. Biblically, this " aura " is described as a " coat of many colours " and as having characterized Joseph, the greatest of the sons of Jacob, in contrast with that patriarch's less morally and spiritually developed sons who were not distinctified by any such coat.

In Masonry the equivalent of the aureole is the symbolic clothing worn by Provincial and Grand Lodge Officers. This is of deep blue, heavily fringed with gold, in correspondence with the deep blue centre and luminous circumference of flame. " His ministers are flames of fire." Provincial and Grand Lodge Officers are drawn from those who are Past Masters in the Craft ; that is, from those who theoretically have attained sanctity, regeneration and Mastership of themselves, and have become joined to the Grand Lodge above where they " shine as the stars."

It follows from all this that the Mason who seriously yields himself to the discipline of the Order is not merely improving his character and chastening his thoughts and desires. He is at the same time unconsciously building up an inner ethereal body which will form his clothing, or covering, when his transitory outer body shall have passed away. " There are celestial bodies and bodies terrestrial ......and as we *have* borne the image of the earthly we also *shall* bear the image of the heavenly." And the celestial body must be built up out of the sublimated properties of the terrestrial one. This is one of the secrets and mysteries of the process of regeneration and self-transmutation, to promote which the Craft was designed. This is the true temple-building that Masonry is concerned with. The Apron being the Masonic symbol of the bodily organism, changes and increasing elaborateness in it as the Mason advances to higher stages in the Craft symbolize (in theory) the actual development that is gradually taking place in his nature.

Moreover, as in the outer heavens of nature the sun, moon and stars exist and function, so in the personal heavens of man there operate metaphysical forces inherent in himself and described by the same terms. In the make-up of each of us exists a psychic magnetic field of various forces, determining our individual temperaments and tendencies and influencing our future. To those forces have also been given the names of " sun," " moon " and planets, and the science of their interaction and outworking was the ancient science of astronomy, or, as it is now more often called astrology, which is one of the liberal arts and sciences recommended to the study of every Mason and the pursuit of which belongs in particular to the Fellow-Craft stage.

THE POSITIONS OF THE OFFICERS OF THE LODGE.

The seven Officers—three principal and three subordinate ones, with an additional minor one serving as a connecting link with the outside world—represent seven aspects or faculties of consciousness psychologically interactive and co-ordinated into a unity so as to constitute a " just and perfect Lodge." As a man, any one of whose faculties is disordered or uncoordinated, is accounted insane, so a Lodge would be imperfect and incapacitated for effective work if its functional mechanism were incomplete.

Seven is universally the number of completeness The time-periods of creation were seven. The spectrum of light consists of seven colours ; the musical scale of seven notes ; our division of time is into weeks of seven days ; our physiological changes run in cycles of seven years. Man himself is a seven-fold organism in correspondence with all these and the normal years of his life are seven multiplied by ten.

The " Master," or Chief Officer, in man is the spiritual principle in him, which is the apex and root of his being and to which all his subsidiary faculties should be subordinate and responsive. When the Master's gavel knocks, those of the Wardens at once repeat the knocks. When the Divine Principle in man speaks in the depth of his being, the remaining portions of his nature should reverberate

101

in sympathy. Without the presence of this Divine Principle in him man would be less than human. Because of its presence in him he can become more than human. By cultivating his consciousness of it he may become unified with it in proportion as he denies and renounces everything in himself that is less than divine. It is the inextinguishable light of a Master Mason which, being immortal and eternal, continues to shine when everything temporal and mortal has disappeared.

The Senior Warden, whilst the Master's chief executive officer, is his antithesis and opposite pole. He personifies the soul, the psychic or animistic principle in man, which, if unassociated with and unillumined by the greater light of the Spirit or Master-principle, has no inherent light of its own at all. At best he in the West can but reflect and transmit that greater light from the East, as the moon receives and reflects sunlight. Wherefore in Masonry his light is spoken of as the moon. In Nature when the moon is not shone upon by the sun it is invisible and virtually non-existent for us ; when it is, it is one of the most resplendent of phenomena. Similarly human intelligence is valuable or negligible according as it is enlightened by the Master-light of the Divine Principle, or merely darkly functioning from its own unillumined energies. In the former case it is the chief executive faculty or transmitting medium of the Supreme Wisdom ; in the latter it can display nothing better than brute-reason.

Midway between the Master-light from the East and the " Moon " in the West is placed the Junior

Warden in the South, symbolizing the third greater light, the " Sun." And, masonically, the " sun " stands for the illuminated human intelligence and understanding, which results from the material brain-mind being thoroughly permeated and enlightened by the Spiritual Principle; it denotes these two in a state of balance and harmonious interaction, the Junior Warden personifying the balance-point or meeting-place of man's natural reason and his spiritual intuition. Accordingly it is he who, as representing this enlightened mental condition, asserts in the Second Degree (which is the degree of personal development where that condition is theoretically achieved) that he has been enabled in that degree to discover a sacred symbol placed in the centre of the building and alluding to the G.G.O.T.U. What is meant is, of course, that the man who has in reality (and not merely ceremonially) advanced to the second degree of self-development has now discerned that God is not outside him, but within him and overshadowing his own " building " or organism; a discovery which he is thereupon urged to follow up with fervency and zeal so that he may more and more closely unify himself with this Divine Principle. This, however, is a process requiring time, effort and self-struggle. The unification is not achieved suddenly. There are found to be obstacles, " enemies " in the way, obstructing it, due to the aspirant's own imperfections and limitations. These must first be gradually overcome, and it is the eradication of these which is alluded to in the sign of the degree, indicating that he desires to cleanse his heart and cast away all evil from it, to purify himself for closer alliance with that pure Light. It is only by this " sun-light," this newly found illumination, that he has become able to see into the depths of his own nature ; and this is the " Sun " which, like Joshua, he prays may " stand still " and its light be retained by him until he has achieved the conquest of all these enemies. The problem of the much discredited biblical miracle of the sun standing still in the heavens disappears when its true meaning is perceived in the light of the interpretation given by the compilers of the Masonic ritual, who well knew that it was not the solar orb that was miraculously stayed in its course in violation of natural law, but that the " sun " in question denotes an enlightened perceptive state experienced by every one who in this " valley of Ajalon " undertakes the task of self-conquest and " fighting the battles of the Lord " against his own lower propensities.

We have now spoken of the Senior and Junior Wardens in their respective psychological significances and as being described as the " Moon " and " Sun." In this connection it is well to point out here that the lights of both Moon and Sun become extinguished in the darkness of the Third Degree. In the great work of self-transformation they are lights and helps up to a point. When that point is reached they are of no further avail ; the grip of each of them proves a slip and the Master-Light, or Divine Principle, alone takes up and completes the regenerative change : " The sun shall be no more thy light by day, neither for brightness shall the moon give light unto thee ; but the Lord shall be unto thee an everlasting light and thy God thy glory ; and the days of thy mourning shall be ended." (*Is. lx.* 19-20).

The three lesser Officers and Tyler, who, with the three principal ones, complete the executive septenary, represent the three greater Officers' energies transmitted into the lower faculties of man's organism. The Senior Deacon, as the Master's adjutant and emissary, forms the link between East and West. The Junior Deacon, as the Senior Warden's adjutant and emissary, forms the link between West and South ; whilst the Inner Guard acts under the immediate control of the Junior Warden and in mutually reflex action with the Outer Guard or contact-point with the outer world of sense-impressions.

The whole seven thus typify the mechanism of human consciousness ; they represent a series of discrete but co-ordinated parts connecting man's outer nature with his inmost Divine Principle and providing the necessary channels for reciprocal action between the spiritual and material poles of his organism.

In other words, and to use an alternative symbol of the same fact, man is potentially a seven-branched golden candlestick. Potentially so, because as yet he has not transmuted the base metals of his nature into gold, or lit up the seven candles or parts of his organism with the Promethean fire of the Divine Principle. Meanwhile that symbol of what is possible to him is offered for his reflection and contemplation, and he may profitably study the

105

description of regenerated, perfected man given in
Revelation 1, 12-20.

To summarize, the seven Officers typify the
following sevenfold parts of the human mechanism :

W.M.   Spirit (*Pneuma*).
S.W.   Soul (*Psyche*).
J.W.   Mind (*Nous*, Intellect).
S.D.   The link between Spirit and Soul.
J.D.   The link between Soul and Mind.
I.G.   The inner sense-nature (astral).
O.G.   The outer sense-nature (physical).

The Greater and Lesser Lights

The purpose of Initiation may be defined as
follows :—it is to stimulate and awaken the Candidate to direct cognition and irrefutable demonstra-
tion of facts and truths of his own being about which
previously he has been either wholly ignorant or
only notionally informed ; it is to bring him into
direct conscious contact with the Realities underlying the surface-images of things, so that, instead
of holding merely beliefs or opinions about himself,
the Universe and God, he is directly and con-
vincingly confronted with Truth itself ; and finally
it is to move him to become the Good and the
Truth revealed to him by identifying himself with
it. (This is of course a gradual process involving
greater or less time and effort in proportion to the
capacity and equipment of the candidate himself.)

The restoration to light of the candidate in the
First Degree is, therefore, indicative of an important
crisis. It symbolizes the first enlargement of perception that, thanks to his own earnest aspirations

and the good offices of the guides and instructors to whom he has yielded himself, Initiation brings him. It reveals to him a threefold symbol, referred to as the three great though emblematic lights in Masonry—the Holy Bible, Square and Compasses in a state of conjunction, the two latter resting on the first-named as their ground or base. As this triple symbol is the first object his outward eye gazes upon after enlightenment, so in correspondence what they emblematize is the first truth his inward eye is meant to recognize and contemplate upon.

He is also made aware of three emblematic lesser lights, described as alluding to the " Sun," " Moon " and " Master of the Lodge," (the psychological significance of which has already been explained in our interpretation of the Officers of the Lodge).

Now the fact is that the candidate can only see the three greater Lights by the help of the three lesser ones. In other words the lesser triad is the instrument by which he beholds the greater one ; it is his own perceptive faculty (subject) looking out upon something larger (object) with which it is not yet identified, just as so small a thing as the eye can behold the expanse of the heavens and the finite mind can contemplate infinitude.

What is implied, then, is that the lesser lights of the candidate's normal finite intelligence are employed to reveal to him the greater lights or fundamental essences of his as yet undeveloped being. A pigmy rudimentary consciousness is being made aware of its submerged source and roots, and placed in sharp contrast with the limitless possibilities available to it when those hidden depths

107

have been developed and brought into function.
The candidate's problem and destiny is to lose
himself to find himself, to unify his lesser with his
greater lights, so that he no longer functions merely
with an elementary reflex consciousness but in
alliance with the All-Conscious with which he has
become identified. In the Royal Arch Degree he
will discover that this identification of the lesser and
greater lights has theoretically become achieved.
The interlaced triangles of lights surrounding the
central altar in that Supreme Degree imply the union
of perceptive faculty with the object of their contemplation ; the blending of the human and the
Divine consciousness.

What then do the three Greater Lights emblematize, and what does their intimate conjunction
connote ?

(1) The written Word is the emblem and
external expression of the unwritten Eternal Word,
the Logos or Substantial Wisdom of Deity out of
which every living soul has emanated and which,
therefore, is the ground or base of human life.
" In the beginning was the Word and the Word
was with God and the Word was God ; without
Him was not anything made that was made ; in
Him was life and the life was the light of men ;
and the light shineth in darkness and the darkness
comprehendeth it not." In an intelligently conducted Lodge the Sacred Volume should lie open
at the first chapter of the Gospel by St. John, the
patron-saint of Masonry, so that it may be these
words that shall meet the candidate's eyes when
restored to light and remind him that the basis of

his being is the Divine Word resident and shining within his own darkness and ignorance, which realize and comprehend not that fact. He has lost all consciousness of that truth, and this dereliction is the " lost Word " of which every Mason is theoretically in search and which with due instruction and his own industry he hopes to find. Finding that, he will find all things, for he will have found God within himself. Let the candidate also reflect that it is the secret motions and promptings of this Word within him that have impelled him to enter the Craft and to seek initiation into light. In the words of a great initiate " thy seeking is the cause of thy finding " ; for the finding is but the final coming to self-consciousness of that inward force which first impelled the quest for light. Hence it is that no one can properly enter the Craft, or hope for real initiation, if he joins the Order from any less motive than that of finding God, the " hid treasure," within himself. His first place of preparation must needs be in the heart, and his paramount desire and heart-hunger must be for that Light which, when attained, is Omniscience coming to consciousness *in him ;* otherwise all ceremonial initiation will be without avail and he will fail even to understand the external symbols and allegories of it.

(2)   The Square, resting upon the Sacred Volume, is the symbol of the human soul as it was generated out of the Divine Word which underlies it. That soul was created " square," perfect, and like everything which proceeded from the Creator's hand was originally pronounced " very good," though

invested with freedom of choice and capacity for
error. The builder's square, however, used as a
Craft symbol, is really an approximation of a triangle
with its apex downwards and base upwards, which
is a very ancient symbol of the soul and psychic
constitution of man and is known as the Water
Triangle.

(3) The Compasses interlaced with the square
are the symbol of the Spirit of the Soul, its functional
energy or Fire. Of itself the soul would be a mere
inert passivity, a negative quantity unbalanced by
a positive opposite. Its active properties are the
product of the union of itself with its underlying
and inspiring Divine basis, as modified by the good
or evil tendencies of the soul itself. God " breathed
into man the breath of life and man became—no
longer a soul, which he was previously—but a *living*
(energizing) soul." This product, or fiery energy,
of the soul is the Spirit of man (a good or evil force
accordingly as he shapes it) and is symbolized by
what has always been known as the Fire Triangle
(with apex upward and base downward), which
symbol is approximately reproduced in the Compasses.

To summarize; the three Greater Lights emblematize the inextricably interwoven triadic groundwork of man's being; (1) the Divine Word or
Substance as its foundation; (2) a passive soul
emanated therefrom; (3) an active spirit or
energizing capacity generated in the soul as the
result of the interaction of the former two. Man
himself therefore (viewed apart from the temporal
body now clothing him) is a triadic unit, rooted in

and proceeding from the basic Divine Substance.

Observe that in the First Degree the points of the Compasses are hidden by the Square. In the Second Degree, one point is disclosed. In the Third both are exhibited. The implication is that as the Candidate progresses, the inertia and negativity of the soul become increasingly transmuted and superseded by the positive energy and activity of the Spirit. The Fire Triangle gradually assumes preponderance over the Water Triangle, signifying that the Aspirant becomes a more vividly living and spiritually conscious being than he was at first.

* * * * * *

OPENING AND CLOSING THE LODGE

FIRST OR ENTERED APPRENTICE DEGREE

If the Lodge with its appointments and officers be a sacramental figure of oneself and of the mechanism of personal consciousness, opening the Lodge in the successive Degrees implies ability to expand, open up and intensify that consciousness in three distinct stages surpassing the normal level applicable to ordinary mundane affairs.

This fact passes unrecognized in Masonic Lodges. The openings and closings are regarded as but so much casual formality devoid of interior purpose or meaning, whereas they are ceremonies of the highest instructiveness and rites with a distinctive purpose which should not be profaned by casual perfunctory performance or without understanding what they imply.

As a flower " opens its Lodge " when it unfolds its petals and displays its centre to the sun which vitalizes it, so the opening of a Masonic Lodge is sacramental of opening out the human mind and heart to God. It is a dramatized form of the psychological processes involved in so doing.

Three degrees or stages of such opening are postulated. First, one appropriate to the apprentice stage of development ; a simple *Sursum corda !* or call to " lift up your hearts ! " above the every-day level of external things. Second, a more advanced opening, adapted to those who are themselves more advanced in the science and capable of greater things than apprentices. This opening is proclaimed to be " upon the square," which the First Degree opening is not. By which is implied that it is one specially involving the use of the psychic and higher intellectual nature (denoted, as previously explained, by the Square or Water Triangle). Third, a still more advanced opening, declared to be " upon the centre," for those of Master Mason's rank, and pointing to an opening up of consciousness to the very centre and depths of one's being.

How far and to what degree any of us is able to open his personal Lodge determines our real position in Masonry and discloses whether we are in very fact Masters, Craftsmen or Apprentices, or only titularly such. Progress in this, as in other things, comes only with intelligent practice and sustained sincere effort. But what is quite over-looked and desirable to emphasize is the power, as an initiatory force, of *an assemblage* of individuals each sufficiently progressed and competent to " open his Lodge " in the sense described. Such an assembly, gathered in one place and acting with a common definite purpose, creates as it were a vortex in the mental and psychical atmosphere into which a newly initiated candidate is drawn. The tension created by their collective energy of thought and will—progressively intensifying as the Lodge is opened in each successive degree, and corres- pondingly relaxing as each Degree is closed—acts and leaves a permanent effect upon the candidate (assuming always that he is equally in earnest and " properly prepared " in an interior sense), inducing a favourable mental and spiritual *rapport* between him and those with whom he seeks to be elevated into organic spiritual membership ; and, further, it both stimulates his perceptivity and causes his mentality to become charged and permeated with the ideas and uplifting influences projected upon him by his initiators.

The fact that a candidate is not admitted within the Lodge-portals without certain assurances, safe- guards and tests, and that even then he is menaced by the sword of the I.G., is an indication that peril to the mental and spiritual organism is recognized as attending the presumptuous engaging in the things with which Initiation deals. As the flaming sword is described as keeping the way to the Tree of Life from those as yet unfitted to approach it, so does the secret law of the Spirit still avenge itself upon those who are unqualified to participate in the knowledge of its mysteries. Hence the command- ment " Thou shalt not take the name of the Lord

thy God in vain," that is by invoking Divine Energy
for unworthy or vain purposes.

Here, and upon the general subject of the signs,
tokens and words employed and communicated in
Initiatory Rites, may usefully be quoted the following
words by a well-informed Mason, who is of course
speaking of them not as the merely perfunctory acts
they are in ordinary Lodges, but as they are when
intelligently employed by those fully instructed in
spiritual science and able to use signs, tokens and
words with dynamic power and real efficiency :—

" The symbols of the Mysteries embodied in the
sign of the Square and Circle constitute the eternal
language of the gods, the same in all worlds, from
all eternity. They have had neither beginning of
years nor end of days. They are contemporary with
time and with eternity. They are the Word of
God, the Divine Logos, articulate and expressed in
forms of language. Each sign possesses a corresponding vocal expression, bodily gesture or mental
intention. This fact is of great importance to the
student of the Wisdom, for in it rests the main
reason of the secrecy and the intense watchfulness
and carefulness of the stewards of the Mysteries
lest the secret doctrines find expression on the lips
or through the action of unfit persons to possess
the secrets. For the secret power of the Mysteries
is within the signs. Any person attaining to natural
and supernatural states by the process of development, if his heart be untuned and his mind withdrawn from the Divine to the human within him,
that power becomes a power of evil instead of a
power of good. An unfaithful initiate, in the degree

of the Mysteries he has attained, is capable, by virtue of his antecedent preparations and processes, of diverting the power to unholy, demoniacal, astral and dangerous uses......The use of the signs, the vocal sounds, physical acts and mental intentions, was absolutely prohibited except under rigorously tested conditions. For instance, the utterance of a symbolical sound, or a physical act, corresponding to a sign belonging to a given degree, in a congregation of an inferior degree, was fatal in its effects. In each degree no initiates who have not attained that degree are admitted to its congregations. Only initiates of that degree, and above it, are capable of sustaining the pressure of dynamic force generated in the spiritual atmosphere and concentrated in that degree. The actual mental ejaculation of a sign, under such circumstances, brought the immediate putting forth of an occult power corresponding to it. In all the congregations of the initiates an Inner Guard was stationed within the sanctuary, chancel or oratory at the door of entrance, with the drawn sword in his hand, to ward off unqualified trespassers and intruders. It was no mere formal or metaphorical performance. It was at the risk of the life of any man attempting to make an entrance if he succeeded in crossing the threshold. Secret signs and passwords and other tests were applied to all who knocked at the door, before admission was granted. The possession of the Mysteries, after initiation, and the use of the signs, either vocally, actionally or ejaculatorily, with " intention " in their use (not as mere mechanical repetition), were attended by occult powers directed to the subjects of their special intention, whether absent or present, or for purposes beneficial to the cause in contemplation." (H. E. Sampson's *Progressive Redemption*, pp. 171-174).

To " open the Lodge " of one's own being to the higher verities is no simple task for those who have closed and sealed it by their own habitual thought-modes, preconceptions and distrust of whatever is not sensibly demonstrable. Yet all these propensities must be eradicated or shut out and the Lodge close tyled against them; they have no part or place in the things of the inward man. Effort and practice also are needed to attain stability of mind, control of emotion and thought, and to acquire interior stillness and the harmony of all our parts. As the formal ceremony of Lodge-opening is achieved only by the organized co-operation of its constituent officers, so the due opening of our inner man to God can only be accomplished by the consensus of all our parts and faculties. Absence or failure of any part invalidates the whole. The W.M. alone cannot open the Lodge; he can only invite his brethren to assist him to do so by a concerted process and the unified wills of his subordinates. So too with opening the Lodge of man's soul. His spiritual will, as master-faculty, summons his other faculties to assist it; " sees that none but Masons are present " by taking care that his thoughts and motives in approaching God are pure; calls all these " brethren " to order to prove their due qualification for the work in hand; and only then, after seeing that the Lodge is properly formed, does he undertake the responsibility of invoking the descent of the Divine blessing and influx upon the unified and dedicated whole.

Of all which the Psalmist writes : " How good and joyful a thing it is for brethren to dwell together in unity..... It is like the precious ointment (anointing) which flows down unto the skirts of the clothing," implying that the Divine influx, when it descends in response to such an invocation, floods and illuminates the entire human organism even to its carnal sense-extremities (which are the " skirts of the clothing " of the soul). Compare also the Christian Master's words : " When thou prayest, enter into thy secret chamber (the Lodge of the soul) and when thou hast shut thy door (by tyling the mind to all outward concerns and thoughts), pray to the Father who seeth in secret, who shall reward thee openly " (by conscious communion).

The foregoing may help both to interpret the meaning and solemn purpose of the Opening in the First Degree, and to indicate the nature of the conditions and spiritual atmosphere that ought to exist when a Lodge is open for business in that Degree. If the Lodge-opening be a real opening in the sense here indicated and not a mere ceremonial form, if the conditions and atmosphere referred to were actually induced at a Masonic meeting, it will be at once apparent that they must needs react powerfully upon a candidate who enters them seeking initiation and spiritual advancement. If he be truly a worthy candidate, properly prepared in his heart and an earnest seeker for the light, the mere fact of his entering such an atmosphere will so impress and awaken his dormant soul-faculties as in itself to constitute an initiation and an indelible memory, whilst the sensitive-plate of his mind thus stimulated will be readily receptive of the ideas projected into it by the assembled brethren who are initiating him and receiving him into spiritual communion with themselves. On the other hand if he be an unworthy or not properly prepared candidate, that atmosphere and those conditions will prove repellent to him and he will himself be the first to wish to withdraw and not to repeat the experience.

The Closing of the First Degree implies the reverse process of the Opening; the relaxing of the inward energies and the return of the mind to its former habitual level. Yet not without gratitude expressed for Divine favours and perceptions received during the period of openness, or without a counsel to keep closed the book of the heart and lay aside the use of its jewels until we are duly called to resume them; since silence and secrecy are essential to the gestation and growth of the inward man. " He who has seen God is dumb."

SECOND OR FELLOW-CRAFT DEGREE

The Opening of the Second Degree presupposes an ability to open up the inner nature and consciousness to a much more advanced stage than is possible to the beginner, who in theory is supposed to undergo a long period of discipline and apprenticeship in the elementary work of self-preparation and to be able to satisfy certain tests that he has done so before being qualified for advancement to the Fellow-craft stage of self-building.

Again that opening may be a personal work for

the individual Mason or a collective work in an
assembly of Fellow-crafts and superior Masons to
pass an Apprentice to Fellow-craft rank.

The title admitting the qualified Apprentice to
a Fellow-craft Lodge is one of great significance,
which ordinarily passes without any observation or
understanding of its propriety. It is said to denote
" in plenty " and to be illustrated by an " ear of
corn near to a fall of water " (which two objects
are literally the meaning of the Hebrew word in
question). It is desirable to observe that this is
meant to be descriptive of the candidate himself,
and of his own spiritual condition. It is he who
is as an ear of corn planted near and nourished by
a fall of water. His own spiritual growth, as
achieved in the Apprentice stage, is typified by the
ripening corn ; the fertilizing cause of its growth
being the down-pouring upon his inner nature of
the vivifying dew of heaven as the result of his
aspiration towards the light.

The work appropriated to the Apprentice Degree
is that of gaining purity and control of his grosser
nature, its appetites and affections. It is symbolized
by working the rough ashlar, as dug from the
quarry, into due shape for building purposes. The
" quarry " is the undifferentiated raw material or
group-soul of humanity from which he has issued
into individuated existence in this world, where his
function is to convert himself into a true die or square
meet for the fabric of the Temple designed by the
Great Architect to be built in the Jerusalem above
out of perfected human souls.

The apprentice-work, which relates to the subdual

119

of the sense-nature and its propensities, being achieved, the next stage is the development and control of the intellectual nature ; the investigation of the " hidden paths of nature (*i.e.*, the human psychological nature) and science " (the *gnosis* of self-knowledge, which, pushed to its limit, the candidate is told " leads to the throne of God Himself " and reveals the ultimate secrets of his own nature and the basic principles of intellectual as distinct from moral truth). It should be noted that the candidate is told that he is now " *permitted to extend his researches* " into these hidden paths. There is peril to the mentality of the candidate if this work is undertaken before the purifications of the Apprentice stage have been accomplished. Hence the permission is not accorded until that preliminary task has been done and duly tested.

The work of the Second Degree is accordingly a purely philosophical work, involving deep psychological self-analysis, experience of unusual phenomena, as the psychic faculties of the soul begin to unfold themselves, and the apprehension of abstract Truth (formerly described as mathematics). This work is altogether beyond both the mental horizon and the capacity of the average modern Mason, though in the Mysteries of antiquity the *Mathesis* (or mental discipline) was an outstanding feature and produced the intellectual giants of Greek philosophy. Hence it is that to-day the Degree is found dull, unpicturesque and unattractive, since psychic experience and intellectual principles cannot be made spectacular and dramatic.

The Ritual runs that our ancient brethren of this

Degree met in the porchway of King Solomon's Temple. This is a way of saying that natural philosophy is the porchway to the attainment of Divine Wisdom; that the study of man leads to knowledge of God, by revealing to man the ultimate divinity at the base of human nature. This study or self-analysis of human nature Plato called Geometry; earth-measuring; the probing, sounding and determining the limits, proportions and potentialities of our personal organism in its physical and psychical aspects. The ordinary natural consciousness is directed outwards; perceives only outward objects; thinks only of an outward Deity separate and away from us. It can accordingly cognize only shadows, images and illusions. The science of the Mysteries directs that that process must be reversed. It says: " Just as you have symbolically shut and close-tyled the door of your Lodge against all outsiders, so you must shut out all perception of outward images, all desire for external things and material welfare, and turn your consciousness and aspirations wholly inward. For the Vital and Immortal Principle—the Kingdom of Heaven—is *within* you; it is not to be found outside you. Like the prodigal son in the parable you have wandered away from it into a far country and lost all consciousness of it. You have come down and down, as by a spiral motion or a winding staircase, into this lower world and imperfect form of exis-tence; coiling around you as you came increasingly thickening vestures, culminating in your outermost dense body of flesh; whilst your mentality has woven about you veil after veil of illusory notions

concerning your real nature and the nature of true
Life. Now the time and the impulse have at last
come for you to turn back to that inward world.
Therefore reverse your steps. Look no longer
outwards, but inwards. Go back up that same
winding staircase. It will bring you to that Centre
of Life and *Sanctum Sanctorum* from which you
have wandered."

When the Psalmist writes " Who will go up the
hill of the Lord? Even he that hath clean hands
and a pure heart," the meaning is identical with
what is implied in the ascent of the inwardly
" winding staircase " of the Second Degree. Preliminary purification of the mind is essential to its
rising to purer realms of being and loftier conscious
states than it has been accustomed to. If " the
secrets of nature and the principles of intellectual
truth " are to become revealed to its view, as the
Degree intends and promises, the mentality must
not be fettered by mundane interests or subject to
disturbance by carnal passions. If it is to " contemplate its own intellectual faculties and trace
them from their development " until they are found
to " lead to the throne of God Himself " and to be
rooted in Deity, it must discard all its former
thought-habits, prejudices and preconceptions, and
be prepared to receive humbly the illumination that
will flood into it from the Light of Divine Wisdom.

For the determined student of the mental
discipline implied by the Second Degree there may
be recommended two most instructive sources of
information and examples of personal experience.
One is the Dialogues of Plato and the writings of

Plotinus and other Neo-Platonists. The other is the records of the classical Christian contemplatives, such as Eckhart or Ruysbroeck or the " Interior Castle " of St. Theresa. The *Phædrus* of Plato, in particular, is an important record by an initiate of the ancient Mysteries of the psychological experiences referred to in the Fellow-Craft Degree.

The subject is too lengthy for further exposition here beyond again indicating that it is in the illumined mental condition attained in this Degree that the discovery is made of the Divine Principle at the centre of our organism ; and that the sign of the Degree is equivalent to a prayer that the sunlight of that exalted state may " stand still " and persist in us until we have effected the overthrow of all our " enemies " and eradicated all obstacles to our union with that Principle.

The reference to our ancient brethren receiving their wages at the porchway of the Temple of Wisdom is an allusion to an experience common to every one in the Fellow-Craft stage of development. He learns that old scores due by him to his fellowmen must be paid off and old wrongs righted, and receives the wages of past sins recorded upon his subconsciousness by that pencil that observes and there records all our thoughts, words and actions. The candidate leading the philosophic life realizes that he is justly entitled to those wages and receives them without scruple or diffidence, knowing himself to be justly entitled to them and only too glad to expiate and purge himself of old offences. For we are all debtors to some one or other for our present position in life, and must

repay what we owe to humanity—perhaps with
tears or adversity—before we straighten our account
with that eternal Justice with which we aspire to
become allied.

THIRD, OR MASTER-MASON'S DEGREE

Before dealing with the opening and closing of
the Third Degree, it should be observed that in
the Lodge symbolism the teaching of the First and
Second Degrees is carried forward into the Third.
The traditional Tracing-Board of the Third Degree
exhibits in combination (1) the chequered floor-
work, (2) the two pillars at the porchway of the
Temple, (3) the winding staircase, and (4) a dormer-
window above the porchway. The brief explanation is given that the chequer-work is for the High
Priest to walk upon and the dormer-window is that
which gave light to it. The entire symbol is but
one comprehensive glyph or pictorial diagram of
the condition of a candidate aspiring to Master
Mason's rank. As high priest of his own personal
temple he must have his bodily nature and its varied
desires under foot. He must have developed
strength of will and character to " walk upon " this
chequer-work and withstand its appeals. He must
also be able to ascend the winding staircase of his
inner nature, to educate and habituate his mentality
to higher conscious states and so establish it there
that he will be unaffected by seductive or affrighting
perceptions that there may meet him. By the
cultivation of this " strength " and the ability to
" establish " himself upon the loftier conscious
levels he co-ordinates the two pillars at the porch-

way of his inmost sanctuary—namely, the physical and psychical supports of his organism—and acquires the " stability " involved in regeneration and requisite to him before passing on to " that last and greatest trial " which awaits him. " In strength will I establish My house that it may stand firm." Man's perfected organism is what is meant by " My house." It was the same organism and the same stability that the Christian Master spoke of in saying " Upon this rock will I build my church and the gates of the underworld shall not prevail against it."

During all the discipline and labour involved in attaining this stability there has shone light on the path from the first moment that his Apprentice's vision was opened to larger truth ; light from the science and philosophy of the Order itself which is proving his " porchway " to the ultimate sanctuary within ; light from friendly helpers and instructors ; above all, light from the sun in his own " heavens," streaming through the " dormer-window " of his illumined intelligence and slowly but surely guiding his feet into the way of peace.

But now the last and greatest trial of his fortitude and fidelity, one imposing upon him a still more serious obligation of endurance, awaits him in the total withdrawal of this kindly light. Hitherto, although guided by that light, he has progressed in virtue of his own natural powers and efforts. Now the time has come when those props have to be removed, when all reliance upon natural abilities, self-will and the normal rational understanding, must be surrendered and the aspirant must abandon

himself utterly to the transformative action of his
Vital and Immortal Principle alone, passively
suffering it to complete the work in entire independence of his lesser faculties. He must " lose his
life to save it " ; he must surrender all that he has
hitherto felt to be his life in order to find life of an
altogether higher order.

Hence the Third Degree is that of mystical
death, of which bodily death is taken as figurative,
just as bodily birth is taken in the First Degree as
figurative of entrance upon the path of regeneration.
In all the Mystery-systems of the past will be found
this degree of mystical death as an outstanding and
essential feature prior to the final stage of perfection
or regeneration. As an illustration one has only
to refer to a sectional diagram of the Great Pyramid
of Egypt, which was so constructed as to be not
merely a temple of initiation, but to record in permanent form the principles upon which regeneration
is attainable. Its entrance passage extends for some
distance into the building as a narrow ascending
channel through which the postulant who desires to
reach the centre must creep in no small discomfort
and restrictedness. This was to emblematise the discipline and up-hill labour of self-purification requisite
in the Apprentice Degree. At a certain point this
restricted passage opens out into a long and lofty
gallery, still upon a steeply rising gradient, up which
the postulant had to pass, but in a condition of ease
and liberty. This was to symbolize the condition
of illumination and expanded intellectual liberty
associated with the Fellow-craft Degree. It ended
at a place where the candidate once more had to

force his way on hands and knees through the smallest aperture of all, one that led to the central chamber in which stood and still stands the great sarcophagus in which he was placed and underwent the last supreme ordeal, and whence he was raised from the dead, initiated and perfected.

The title of admission communicated to the candidate for the Third Degree is noteworthy, as also the reason for it. It is a Hebrew name, said to be that of the first artificer in metals and to mean " in worldly possessions." Now it will be obvious that the name of the first man who worked at metal-making in the ordinary sense can be of no possible interest or concern to us to-day, nor has the information the least bearing upon the subject of human regeneration. It is obviously a veil of allegory concealing some relevant truth. Such it will be found to be upon recognizing that Hebrew Biblical names represent not persons, but personifications of spiritual principles, and that Biblical history is not ordinary history of temporal events but a record of eternally true spiritual facts. The matter is, therefore, interpretable as follows : We know from the teaching of the Entered Apprentice Degree what " money and metals " are in the Masonic sense, and that they represent the attractive power of temporal possessions, and earthly belongings and affections of whatever description. We know too that from the attraction and seductiveness of these things, and even from the desire for them, it is essential to be absolutely free if one desires to attain that Light and those riches of Wisdom for which the candidate professes to long. Not that it is necessary for him to become literally and physically dispossessed of worldly possessions, but it is essential that he should be so utterly detached from them that he cares not whether he owns any or not and is content, if need be, to be divested of them entirely if they stand in the way of his finding " treasure in heaven " ; for so long as he clings to them or they exercise control over him, so long will his initiation into anything better be deferred.

It follows then that it is the personal soul of the candidate himself which is the " artificer in metals " referred to, and which during the whole of its physical existence has been engaged in trafficking with " metals." Desire for worldly possessions, for sensation and experience in this outward world of good and evil, brought the soul into this world. There it has woven around itself its present body of flesh, every desire and thought being an " artificer " adding something to or modifying its natural encasement. The Greek philosophers used to teach that souls secrete their bodies as a snail secretes his shell, and our own poet Spenser truly wrote :

> " For of the soul the body form doth take,
> And soul is form and doth the body make."

If, then, desire for physical experience and material things brought the soul into material conditions (as is also indicated in the great parable of the Prodigal Son), the relinquishing of that desire is the first necessary step to ensure its return to the condition whence it first emanated. Satiation with and consequent disgust at the " husks " of things instigated the Prodigal Son to aspire to return home. Similar repletion and revolt drives many a man to lose all desire for external things and to seek for peace within himself and there redirect his energies in quest of possessions which are abiding and real. This is the moment of his true " conversion," and the moment when he is ripe for initiation into the hidden Mysteries of his own being. The First and Second Degrees of Masonry imply that the candidate has undergone lengthy discipline in the renunciation of external things and the cultivation of desire for those that are within. But, notwithstanding that he has passed through all the discipline of those Degrees, he is represented at the end of them as being still not entirely purified and to be still " in worldly possessions " in the sense that a residue of attraction by them and reliance upon himself lingers in his heart ; and it is these last subtle close-clinging elements of " base metal " in him that need to be eradicated if perfection is to be attained. The ingrained defects and tendencies of the soul as the result of all its past habits and experiences are not suddenly eliminated or easily subdued. Self-will and pride are very subtle in their nature and may continue to deceive their victim long after he has purged himself of grosser faults. As Cain was the murderer of Abel, so every taint of base metal in oneself debases the gold of the Vital and Immortal Principle. It must be renounced, died to and transmuted in the crucial process of the Third Degree. Hence it is that the candidate is entrusted with a name that designates himself at this stage and that indicates that he is still " in worldly possessions;" that is, that some residue of the spirit of this world yet lingers in him which it is necessary to eliminate from his nature before he can be raised to the sublime degree of Master.

Examination of the text of the opening and closing of the Lodge in the Third Degree discloses the whole of the philosophy upon which the Masonic system is reared. It indicates that the human soul has originated in the eternal East—that "East" being referable to the world of Spirit and not to any geographical direction—and that thence it has directed its course towards the "West"—the material world which is the antipodes of the spiritual and into which the soul has wandered. Its purpose in so journeying from spiritual to physical conditions is declared to be the quest and recovery of something it has lost, but which by its own industry and suitable instruction it hopes to find. From this it follows that the loss itself occurred prior to its descent into this world, otherwise that descent would not have been necessary. What it is that has been lost is not explicitly declared, but is implied and is stated to form "the genuine secrets of a Master Mason." It is the loss of a word, or rather of The Word, the Divine Logos, or basic root and essence of our own being. In other words the soul of man has ceased to be God-conscious and has degenerated into the limited terrestrial consciousness of the ordinary human being. It is in the condition spoken of in the cosmic parable of Adam when extruded from Eden, an exile from the Divine Presence and condemned to toil and trouble. The quest after this lost Word is declared by the

Wardens to have been so far abortive, and to have resulted in the discovery, not of that Reality, but of substitutional images of it. All which implies that, in the strength of merely his natural temporal intelligence, man can find and know nothing more in this world than shadows, images and phenomenal forms of realities which abide eternally and noumenally in the world of Spirit to which his temporal faculties are at present closed. Yet there remains a way of regaining consciousness of that higher world and life. It is by bringing into function a now dormant and submerged faculty resident at the depth and centre of his being. That dormant faculty is the Vital and Immortal Principle which exists as the central point of the circle of his individuality. As the outward Universe is the externalized projection of an indwelling immanent Deity, so is the outward individual man the externalization and diffusion of an inherent Divine germ, albeit perverted and distorted by personal self-will and desire which have dislocated and shut off his consciousness from his root of being. Recover contact with that central Divine Principle by a voluntary renunciation of the intervening obstructions and inharmonious elements in oneself, and man at once ceases to be merely the rationalized animal he now is and becomes grafted upon a new and Divine life-principle, a sharer of Omniscience and a co-operator with Deity. He recovers the lost and genuine secrets of his own being and has for ever finished with substitutions, shadows and simulacra of Reality. He reaches a point and lives from a centre from which no Master Mason can ever err or will ever again desire to err, for it is the end, object and goal of his existence.

Meanwhile, until actual recovery of that lost secret, man must put up with its substitutions and regard these as sacramental of concealed realities, contact with which will be his great reward if he submits himself to the conditions upon which alone he may discover them. The existence of those realities and the regimen essential to their enjoyment are inculcated by Masonry as they have been by every other initiatory Order of the past, and it is for the fact that this knowledge is and always has been conserved in the world, so as to be ever available for earnest aspirants towards it, that gratitude is expressed to the Grand Master of all for having never left Himself, or the way of return to Him, without witness in this outer world.

As much has been said about the Ceremony of the Third Degree in other papers it is unnecessary here to expound it further. It may be stated, however, that it alone constitutes the Masonic Initiation. The First and Second Degrees are, strictly, but preparatory stages leading up to Initiation; they are not the Initiation itself; they but prescribe the purification of the bodily and mental nature necessary to qualify the candidate for the end which crowns the whole work. To those unacquainted with what is really involved in actual as distinct from merely ceremonial initiation, and who have no notion of what initiation meant in the old schools of Wisdom and still means for those who understand the theory of Regenerative Science, it is well nigh impossible to convey any idea of its process or its results. The modern Mason, however high in titular rank, is as little qualified to understand the subject as the man who has never entered a Lodge. " To become initiated (or perfected)," says an old authority, Plutarch, " involves dying " ; not a physical death, but a moral way of dying in which the soul is loosened from the body and the sensitive life, and becoming temporarily detached therefrom is set free to enter the world of Eternal Light and Immortal Being. This, after most drastic preliminary disciplines, was achieved in a state of trance and under the supervision of duly qualified Masters and Adepts who intromitted the candidate's liberated soul into its own interior principles until it at last reached the Blazing Star or Glory at its own Centre, in the light of which it simultaneously knew itself and God, and realized their unity and the " points of fellowship " between them. Then it was that, from this at once awful and sublime experience, the initiated soul was brought back to its bodily encasement again and " reunited to the companions of its former toils," to resume its temporal life, but with conscious realization of Life Eternal superadded to its knowledge and its powers. Then only was it entitled to the name of Master Mason. Then only could it exclaim, in the words of another initiate (Empedocles), " Farewell, all earthly allies ; henceforth am I no mortal wight, but an immortal angel, ascending up into Divinity and reflecting upon that likeness of it which I have found in myself. "

The " secrets " of Freemasonry and of initiation are largely connected with this process of intro-

133

version of the soul to its own Centre, and beyond this brief reference to the subject it is inexpedient here to say more. But in confirmation of what has been indicated it may be useful to refer to the 23rd Psalm, in which the Hebrew Initiates speak of both the supreme experience of being passed through " the valley of the shadow of death " and the preliminary phases of mental preparation for that ordeal. Stripping that familiar psalm of the gorgeous metaphor given it in the beautiful Biblical translation, its real meaning may be paraphrased and explained for Masonic students as follows :—

" The Vital and Immortal Principle within me is my Initiator ; and is all-sufficient to lead me to God.

It has made me lie down (in self-discipline and humiliation) in " green pastures " of meditation and mental sustenance.

It has led me beside " still waters " of contemplation (as distinct from the " rough sea of passion " of my natural self).

It is restoring my soul (reintegrating it out of chaos and disorder).

Even when I come to pass through the valley of deadly gloom (my own interior veils of darkness) I will fear no evil ; for It is with me (as a guiding star) ; Its directions and disciplines will safeguard me.

It provides me with the means of overcoming my inner enemies and weaknesses ; It anoints my intelligence with the oil of wisdom ; the cup of my mind brims over with new light and consciousness.

The Divine Love and Truth, which I shall find face to face at my centre, will be a conscious presence to me all the days of my temporal life ; and thereafter I shall dwell in a " house of the Lord " (a glorified spiritual body) for ever."

The Third Degree is completed in, and can only be more fully expounded by reference to, the Holy Royal Arch Ceremony. A separate further paper will, therefore, be devoted to that Ceremony.

THE MASONIC APRON

From what has been said in these pages the full significance of the Apron will now be perceived and may be summarized thus :—

1. The Apron is the symbol of the corporeal vesture and condition of the soul (not so much of the temporal physical body, as of its permanent invisible corporeity which will survive the death of the mortal part).

2. The soul fabricates its own body or " apron " by its own desires and thoughts (see *Genesis III*, 7, " they made themselves aprons ") and as these are pure or impure so will that body be correspondingly transparent and white, or dense and opaque.

3. The investiture of the candidate with the Apron in each Degree by the Senior Warden as the Master's delegate for that purpose is meant to inculcate this truth; for the Senior Warden represents the soul which, in accordance with its own spirituality, automatically clothes *itself* with its own self-made vesture in a way that marks its own progress or regress.

135

4. The unadorned white Apron of the First Degree indicates the purity of soul contemplated as being attained in that Degree.

5. The pale blue rosettes added to the Apron in the Second Degree indicate that progress is being made in the science of regeneration and that the candidate's spirituality is beginning to develop and bud through. Blue, the colour of the sky, is traditionally associated with devotion to spiritual concerns.

6. In the Third Degree still further progress is emblematized by the increased blue adornments of the Apron, as also by its silver tassels and the silver serpent used to fasten the apron-strings. In the First and Second Degrees no metal has appeared upon the Apron. The candidate has been theoretically divesting himself of all base metals and transmuting them into spiritual riches. With Mastership he has attained an influx of those riches under the emblem of the tassels of silver, a colourless precious metal always associated with the soul, as gold by reason of its supreme value and warm colour is associated with Spirit. The silver serpent is the emblem of Divine Wisdom knitting the soul's new-made vesture together.

7. The pale blue and silver of the Master Mason's Apron become intensified in the deep blue and gold ornamentation worn by the Grand Lodge Officers, who in theory have evolved to still deeper spirituality and transmuted themselves from silver into fine gold. " The king's daughter (the soul) is all glorious within ; her clothing is of wrought gold," *i.e.*, wrought or fabricated by her own spiritual energies.

A Prayer at Lodge Closing

O Sovereign and Most Worshipful of all Masters, who, in Thy infinite love and wisdom, hast devised our Order as a means to draw Thy children nearer Thee, and hast so ordained its Officers that they are emblems of Thy seven-fold power;

Be Thou unto us an Outer Guard, and defend us from the perils that beset us when we turn from that which is without to that which is within;

Be Thou unto us an Inner Guard, and preserve our souls that desire to pass within the portal of Thy holy mysteries;

Be unto us the Younger Deacon, and teach our wayward feet the true and certain steps upon the path that leads to Thee: Be Thou also the Elder Deacon, and guide us up the steep and winding stairway to Thy throne;

Be unto us the Lesser Warden, and in the meridian sunlight of our understanding speak to us in sacraments that shall declare the splendours of Thy unmanifested light;

Be Thou also unto us the Greater Warden, and in the awful hour of disappearing light, when vision fails and thought has no more strength, be with us still, revealing to us, as we may bear them, the hidden mysteries of Thy shadow;

And so, through light and darkness, raise us, Great Master, till we are made one with Thee, in the unspeakable glory of Thy presence in the East.

So mote it be.

Chapter IV.

THE HOLY ROYAL ARCH
OF JERUSALEM.

FREEMASONRY, under the English Constitution, reaches its climax and conclusion
in the Order of the Holy Royal Arch. There
exists a variety of other degrees ramifying from
the main stem of the Masonic system which either
elaborate side-points of its doctrine or re-express
its teachings in alternative symbolism. These,
while of greater or less merit and interest, are
beyond our present consideration, and, indeed, are
superfluities tending rather to diffuse the student's
attention than to deepen his insight into the central
purpose of the Craft. The taking of additional
higher degrees may be indulged in almost indefinitely,
but to what purpose if the initial ones, which
contain all that is necessary for the understanding
of the subject, remain imperfectly assimilated?
It is a fallacy to suppose that the multiplying
of degrees will result in the discovery of important
arcane secrets which one has failed to find in
the rites of the Craft and the Royal Arch. The higher
degrees indeed illustrate truths of much interest
and often set forth with impressive ceremonial
beauty, the appreciation of which will be the greater
after and not before the meaning of the preliminary
ones has been thoroughly absorbed; whilst the
pursuit of " secrets " is certain to prove illusory,
for the only secrets worth the name or the finding
are those incommunicable ones which discover
themselves within the personal consciousness of the

seeker who is in earnest to translate ceremonial representation into facts of spiritual experience.

It was accordingly a sound instinct that prompted those who settled the present constitution of the Order to exclude these supplementary refinements and to declare that " Masonry consists of the three Craft Degrees and the Holy Royal Arch and no more," for within that compass is exhibited, or at least outlined, the entire process of human regeneration ; so that after the Royal Arch there really remains nothing more to be said, although what has been said is of course capable of elaboration.

The completeness of regeneration theoretically postulated in those four stages is marked, it should be observed, by the very significant expression used in connection with a Royal Arch Chapter, which is interpreted as meaning " My people having obtained mercy," which in its further analysis signifies that all the parts and faculties (" people ") of the candidate's organism have at last, and as the result of his previous discipline and ordeals, become sublimated and integrated in a new quality and higher order of life than that previously enjoyed in virtue of his merely temporal nature. In a word, he has become regenerated. He has achieved the miracle of " squaring the circle "—a metaphorical expression for regeneration, as shall be explained presently.

Although but an expansion and completion of the Third Degree, of which at one time it formed part, there were good reasons for detaching the Royal Arch portion from what now forms the Degree of Master Mason. The two parts in combination made an inconveniently long rite, whilst a change in the symbolic appointments and officers of the temple of initiation was necessary, as the ceremony proceeded, to give appropriate spectacular representation to the further points calling for expression. Despite this re-arrangement the Royal Arch is the natural conclusion and fulfilment of the Third Degree. The latter inculcates the necessity of mystical death and dramatizes the process of such death and revival therefrom into newness of life. The Royal Arch carries the process a stage farther, by showing its fulfilment in the " exaltation " or apotheosis of him who has undergone it. The Master Mason's Degree might be said to be represented in the terms of Christian theology by the formula " He suffered and was buried and rose again," whilst the equivalent of the exaltation ceremony is " He ascended into heaven."

The Royal Arch Degree seeks to express that new and intensified life to which the candidate can be raised and the exalted degree of consciousness that comes with it. From being conscious merely as a natural man and in the natural restricted way common to every one born into this world, he becomes exalted (whilst still in his natural flesh) to consciousness in a supernatural and illimitable way. As has been said in previous papers, the purpose of all initiation is to lift human consciousness from lower to higher levels by quickening the latent spiritual potentialities in man to their full extent through appropriate discipline. No higher level of attainment is possible than that in which the human merges in the Divine consciousness and knows as

God knows. And that being the level of which the Order of the Royal Arch treats ceremonially, it follows that Masonry as a sacramental system reaches its climax and conclusion in that Order.

As has also been already shown, to attain that level involves as its essential prerequisite the total abnegation, renouncement and renovation of one's original nature, the surrender of one's natural desires, tendencies and preconceptions, and the abandonment and nullifying of one's natural self-will, by such a habitual discipline and self-denial and gradual but vigorous opposition to all these as will cause them gradually to atrophy and die down. " He that loveth his life shall lose it, and he that hateth his life in this world shall keep it unto life eternal. Except a corn of wheat fall into the ground and die, it abideth alone ; but if it die it bringeth forth much fruit." As with a seed of wheat, so with man. If he persists in clinging to the present natural life he knows, if he refuses to recognize that a higher quality of life is here and now possible to him, or is unwilling to make the necessary effort to attain it, he " abideth alone," gets nowhere, and only frustrates his own spiritual evolution. But if he is willing to " die " in the sense indicated, if he will so re-orientate his will and silence his natural energies and desires as to give the Vital and Immortal Principle within him the chance to assert itself and supersede them, then from the disintegrated material of his old nature that germ of true life will spring into growth in him and bear much fruit, and by the stepping-stones of initiation he will rise from his dead self to higher things than he can otherwise experience.

This necessity of self-dying—not, we repeat, the physical death of the body but a mystical death-in-life of everything except the body—is the first and fundamental fact to be grasped before one may hope to realize or even to understand the mystery of the Royal Arch Degree. " *Mors janua vitae* "; death to self is the portal to true life. There is no other way. It is the unescapable law and condition of the soul's progress.

But since it is a process involving a " most serious trial of fortitude and fidelity " and a grapple with oneself from which the timorous and self-diffident may well shrink, the Mystery-systems have always exhibited an example for the instruction, encouragement and emulation of those prepared to make the attempt and the necessary sacrifice. To hearten them to the task the Initiatory Colleges have held up a prototype in the person of some great soul who has already trodden the same path and emerged triumphant therefrom. It matters nothing whether the prototype be one whose historic actuality and identity can be demonstrated, or whether he can be regarded only as legendary or mythical ; the point being not to teach a merely historical fact, but to enforce a spiritual principle. In Egypt the prototype was Osiris, who was slain by his malignant brother Typhon, but whose mangled limbs were collected in a coffer from which he emerged reintegrated and divinized. In Greece the prototype was Bacchus, who was torn to pieces by the Titans. Baldur in Scandinavia and Mithra in Græco-Roman Europe were similar prototypes. In Masonry the prototype is Hiram Abiff, who met his death as the result of a conspiracy by a crowd of workmen of whom there were three principal ruffians. In the Christian and chief of all systems, since it comprehends and re-expresses all the others, the greatest of the Exemplars died at the hands of the mob, headed also by three chief ruffians, Judas, Caiaphas and Pilate. If in Masonry the mystical death is dramatized more realistically than the resurrection that follows upon it, that resurrection is nevertheless shown in the " raising " of the candidate to the rank of Master Mason and his " reunion with the companions of former toils," implying the reintegration and resumption of all his old faculties and powers in a sublimated state, just as the limbs of the risen Osiris were said to reunite into a new whole and as the Christian Master withdrew His mutilated body from the tomb and reassumed it, transmuted into one of supernatural substance and splendour.

We have, therefore, now to consider how the Royal Arch Degree exhibits the attainment of a new order of life. But it may be as well to say in advance that for those unhabituated to looking beyond surface-values and material meanings the exposition about to be given, dealing as it will with the profound spiritual truths and advanced psychological experience allegorized by the external ceremonial, is likely to present some difficulty of comprehension and acceptance. The Royal Arch, however, would not be the Supreme Degree it is did it not move upon a supremely high level of thought and instruction. It was not compiled to accommodate the elementary intelligence theoretically characterizing the philosophically untrained neophyte. It presupposes that its candidate has passed through a long, strenuous period of purification and mental discipline, in the course of which his understanding has become very considerably widened and deepened, whilst his fidelity to the high inward Light which has conducted him safely so far, has induced in him a humility and docility fitting him for what still awaits him—the attainment of that Wisdom which is concealed from this world's wise and prudent, but is revealed unto babes. It is a rite of initiation dealing less with his gross corporeal nature and his ordinary temporal mentality (which have been the subject of purification in the earlier degrees) than with the higher reaches and possibilities of his understanding and consciousness. As it is, what can be said here can at best be but a partial and incomplete exposition of a theme calling rather for disciplined imagination and reverent reflection than for reasoned argument. Certain things must perforce be omitted from explanation entirely, whilst others are mentioned with diffidence and at the risk of their being misunderstood or rejected by such as do not yet realize that in these matters " the letter killeth, the spirit vivifieth " and that " spiritual truths must be spiritually discerned."

Before interpreting the Ceremony itself it is desirable first to indicate four noteworthy features connected with this Supreme Order and distinctifying it from the three grades leading to it. In speaking even of these incidentals the beforementioned difficulties of both exposition and apprehension will already make themselves felt.

First, no one can be received into a Chapter without first having attained Master Mason's rank.

144

Second, the circular symbol of the Grand Geometrician, which in the Second Degree shone high above in the ceiling of the Temple, and in the Third Degree had moved downwards and burned as a glimmering ray in the East to guide the candidate's feet into the way of peace, has now descended completely to the chequer-work floor, where it rests as the centre and cubical focus of the entire organism and bears the Sacred and Ineffable Name, as also those of Solomon and the two Hirams.

Third, the constitution of the Assembly is no longer one of seven officers, but of nine, who are grouped in three triads about the Central Sacred Symbol.

Fourth, the Assembly, regarded as a unity, is no longer designated a Lodge, but a Chapter.

The first of these points—that none but a Master Mason can enter the Royal Arch—has already been accounted for. It is not feasible, nor is it within the law governing the process of spiritual evolution, for any who has not experienced the stage of mystical death to have experience of that which lies beyond that death. As an unborn physical infant can know nothing of this world, in which nevertheless it exists, until actually initiated into it by birth, so the embryonic spiritual child cannot be born into conscious function upon the plane of the Spirit until it has become entirely detached from the enfolding carnal matrix and tendencies to which it has been habituated.

The second and third points can be considered together. The re-arrangement of the factors constituting the ceremonial temple are symbolic of a structural re-arrangement which has occurred in the candidate's own psychical organization. This has undergone a repolarization as the result of the descent into it of that high central Light which at first but shone as it were in his "heavens," afar off and above him, illumining the dormer-window of his natural intelligence. Consider deeply what this change implies. The Day-star from on high has now visited him; the fontal source of all consciousness has descended into the very chequer-work material of his transient physical organism, not merely permeating it temporarily with light, but taking root and becoming grafted there substantially and permanently. In theological language, God has become man, and man has become divinized, in virtue of this descent and union. In Masonic terms, the Vital and Immortal Principle resident in the candidate has at last superseded his temporal life-principle and established him upon a new centre of incorruptible life. Now, and perhaps only now, becomes thoroughly appreciable the necessity for the earlier purifications, discipline, self-crucifixion and death of all the lower nature. How could the purity of the Divine Essence tabernacle in the coarse body of the sensualist? How could the Eternal Wisdom unfold its treasures in a mind benighted or caring for nothing but base metals and material pursuits? How could the Universal Will co-operate with and function through the man whose petty personal will blocks its channel, antagonizing it at every turn with his selfish preferences and disordered desires? A Master Mason, then, in the full sense of the term, is no longer an ordinary man, but a divinized man; one

in whom the Universal and the personal consciousness have come into union. Obviously the quality
of life and consciousness of such an one must differ
vastly from that of other men. His whole being is
differently qualitated and geared upon another
centre. That new centre is described as the Grand
Geometrician of man's personal universe, inasmuch
as its action upon the organism of whoever surrenders
himself to its influence causes a redisposition of
functional and conscious faculty. The knowledge
of this fact was with the wise ancients the true and
original science of Geometry (literally " earth-
measuring " ; determining the occult potentialities
of the human earth or temporal organism under
spiritual stresses). " God geometrizes " wrote
Plato, with intimate knowledge of the subject.
Many of the Euclidean and Pythagorean theorems,
now regarded merely as mathematical demonstra-
tions, were originally expressions, veiled in
mathematical glyphs, of the esoteric science of
soul-building or true Masonry. The well-known
47th Proposition of the First Book of Euclid is an
example of this and in consequence has come
(though few modern Masons could explain why)
to be inscribed upon the Past Master's official jewel.
Again, the squaring of the circle—that problem
which has baffled so many modern mathematicians
—is an occult expression signifying that Deity,
symbolized by the all-containing circle, has attained
form and manifestation in a " square " or human
soul. It expresses the mystery of the Incarnation,
accomplished within the personal soul.

Under the stress then of the Geometrizing

Principle now found symbolically integrated within the candidate's temporal organism, a re-distribution of his component powers has become effected. His repolarized condition is symbolized by an equilateral triangle with a point at its centre, and such a triangle will be found, worked in gold, upon the sash worn by the Companions of the Order. The significance of this triangle is that the tripartite aspects of him who wears it (that is, the spiritual, psychical and physical parts of him) now stand equalized and equilibrated around their common Life-Principle at the centre, fitted and equipped for Its purpose. Yet each of these three divisions, though in itself unitary, is philosophically triadic in composition when subjected to intellectual analysis. " Every monad is the parent of a triad " is another maxim of the Ancients, who anticipated the modern Hegelian proposition of metaphysics that thesis, antithesis and synthesis are the essential ingredients of a given truth. Hence it comes about that the three aspects of *each* of the three sides of our equilateral triangle are ceremonially personified by the nine officers of the Chapter—three in the East representing the spiritual side, three in the West figuring the soul or psychical side, and three subordinate links connecting these other two. (These will be further and more conveniently treated of later when the symbolic nature of the officers is dealt with).

The fourth point to be noticed was the change of designation from " Lodge " to " Chapter." The word " Chapter " derives from *Caput*, head. The reason for the change of name lies, however, much deeper than in the fact that the Royal Arch stands at the head or summit of the Craft. It has reference in a twofold way to the capitular rank and consciousness of the Arch Mason himself. In virtue of his headship or supremacy over his material nature he has passed beyond mere Craftwork and governing the Lodge of his lower nature, which he has now made the docile instrument and servant of his spiritual self. Henceforth his energies are employed primarily upon the spiritual plane. The " head " of the material organism of man is the spirit of man, and this spirit consciously conjoined with the Universal Spirit is Deity's supreme instrument and vehicle in the temporal world. Such a man's physical organism and brain have become sublimated and keyed up to a condition and an efficiency immensely in advance of average humanity. Physiological processes are involved which cannot be discussed here, beyond saying that in such a man the entire nervous system contributes to charge certain ganglia and light up certain brain-centres in a way of which the ordinary mind knows nothing. The nervous system provides the storage-batteries and conductive medium of the Spirit's energies just as telegraph wires are the media for transmitting electrical energy. But the true Master Mason, in virtue of his mastership, knows how to control and apply those energies. They culminate and come to self-consciousness in his head, in his intelligence. And in this respect we may refer to a very heavily veiled Scriptural testimony, the import of which goes quite unperceived to the uninstructed reader. The Gospels record that the Passion of the Great

Exemplar and Master concluded " at the place
called Golgotha in the Hebrew tongue ; that is, the
place of a skull " ; that is to say it terminated in the
head or seat of intelligence and in a mystery of the
spiritual consciousness. The same truth is also
testified to, though again under veils of symbolic
phrasing, in the reference to the sprig of acacia
planted at the head of the grave of the Masonic
Grand Master and prototype, Hiram Abiff. The
grave is the candidate's soul ; the sprig of acacia
typifies the latent *akasa* (to use an Eastern term) or
divine germ planted in that soil and waiting to
become quickened into activity in his intelligence,
the " head " of that plane. When that sprig of
acacia blooms at the head of his soul's sepulchre,
he will understand at one and the same moment
the mystery of Golgotha, the mystery of the death
of Hiram, and the meaning of the Royal Arch
ceremony of exaltation. It is a mystery of spiritual
consciousness, the efflorescence of the mind in God,
the opening up of the human intelligence in conscious
association with the Universal and Omniscient Mind.
It is for this reason that the cranium or skull is given
prominence in the Master Mason's Degree.

With this premised we proceed to considering
the Ceremony of Exaltation.

THE CEREMONY OF EXALTATION

Again the candidate is in a state of darkness.
But the reason of this darkness differs entirely from
that which existed at the Entered Apprentice stage.
Then he was but an ignorant beginner upon the
quest, making his first irregular benighted efforts

towards the light.   Now, he has long passed beyond
that stage ; he comes with all the qualifications and
equipment of a Master Mason.   Long ago he found
the light he first sought, and for long he has been
directing his steps and nourishing his growth by
its rays.   And more ; after all this intimacy with
it he has known it recede from him and disappear
in the great ordeal of dereliction of the Third Degree,
when, in the " dark night of the soul " and utter
helplessness of all his powers, he learned how strength
could be perfected out of weakness by the potent
efficacy of the Vital and Immortal Principle within
him, in whose presence the darkness and the light
are both alike.   His present initial deprivation of
light is the darkness of the Third Degree carried
over into this further experience.   It betokens
rather a momentary failure to adjust his perception
to the new quality of life he is now entering upon,
just as a new-born child is unable at first to co-
ordinate its sight to objects before it.   For a while,
but only for a brief while, the candidate feels
himself in darkness ; but he is really blinded rather
by excess of light than by lack of it.

In this condition he undertakes the opening out
of a certain place which he proceeds to enter and
explore, keeping touch meanwhile with his companions by a cord or life-line.   The symbolism of
all this is singularly rich in allusion to certain
interior processes of introspection well defined in
the experience of the contemplative mystics and well
attested in their records.   The place entered
emblematizes once again the material and psychical
organism, a dense compact of material particles

coating the more tenuous interior spirit of man as a shell surrounds the contents of an egg. " Roll away the stone," it will be recalled, was the first injunction of the Master at the raising of Lazarus. This obstruction removed, the psychical organism becomes detached from the physical and the mind is free to become introverted and work exploratively upon its own ground, to search the contents of its own unplumbed depths, to probe deeper and deeper into itself, eradicating defects and removing rubble, pushing in and in by the energy of a persistent will, yet retaining contact the while with the outer physical nature by a subtle filament or life-line which prevents their entire separation. The position is the same as when the body sleeps whilst the mind is dreaming and vividly active, save that in dreams the will is not functioning as a consciously directive instrument as is hypothetically the case with one who, having attained Mastership, has all his faculties under volition and control. Yet all this interior work, so rapidly summarized and symbolically enacted in the Ceremony, is not the work of a day nor the casual task of a weakling. The ancients referred to it as the twelve labours of Hercules, whilst its arduousness is further graphically described by the initiate poet Virgil in the sixth Æneid and by more recent illuminates. Nor, even when its nature is fully apprehended, is it a work to be lightly undertaken. Throughout the Ceremony the utmost humility is enjoined upon the candidate as the essential qualification for entering upon this process of self-exploration. He is bidden to draw nigh to the Centre, but to halt and make obeisance at three several stages, at each of which he is told he is approaching more nearly to that central Essence, that holy ground of his being upon which only the humble can walk, that " earth " which only the meek shall inherit.

It is in this state that the introverted mind, groping for its own foundation and centre, reaches at length the bedrock of its being. As the symbolic ceremony exhibits the grasping of an emblem embodying the Word of Life, so literally and in fact the questing mind, in coming upon the Vital and Immortal Principle animating it, " lays hold on Eternal Life." It discovers the Lost Word, the divine root of its being, from which it has hitherto been so long dissociated. It fails to realize the fact at first, for " the Light shineth in darkness and the darkness comprehendeth it not."   Presently that darkness will disappear ; when " the day (the new consciousness) dawns and the shadows (the old mentality) flee away."

Therefore it is that this work of the introverted mind and the discovery it makes, are exhibited as taking place darkly and amid subterranean gloom. There remains, therefore, one concluding psychological process—to extrovert that knowledge and bring it forward into formalized brain-consciousness, so that what the spirit and the soul already know interiorly the outer mind may also know exteriorly. Subjective awareness does not become knowledge until it has been cerebrated and passed through the alembic of the brain and the logical understanding. When it has so passed through and become formalized, a reciprocal and reflex action between the inner

153

and outer natures is set up resulting in the illumination of the whole. This extroversion of subjective perceptions is symbolically achieved by the return of the candidate from the subterranean depths to the surface and there rejoining his former companion-sojourners and effecting a unification of all his component parts.

It is then that the Mystery is consummated. The Great Light breaks. The Vital and Immortal Principle comes to self-consciousness in him. The Glory of the Lord is revealed to and in him, and all his flesh sees it.

So far as it is possible for symbolic ceremonial to portray it this consummation is represented by the restoration to light and the revelation that then meets the candidate's gaze. His condition differs now from any that has preceded it. It is not merely one of illumination *by* the Supernal Light. It is one of identification *with* It. He and It have become one, as a white-hot iron is indistinguishable from the furnace-flame engulfing it. At the outset of his Masonic quest the predominant wish of his heart was Light. The impulse was not his own; it was that of the Light Itself—the primal Light of light, the Divine Substantial Word—seeking self-development in him. Consciousness is that Light become self-perceptive by polarization within an efficient physiological organism. Man provides the only organism adapted to the attainment of that self-perception; but only when that organism is purified and prepared sufficiently for the achievement. In the Royal Arch that achievement is hypothetically effected.

The condition attained by the illumined candidate
is the equivalent of what in Christian theology is
known as Beatific Vision and in the East as *Samadhi.*
It is also spoken of as universal or cosmic
consciousness, since the percipient, transcending
all sense of personal individualization, time and
space, is co-conscious with all that is. He has
entered the bliss and peace surpassing that
temporal understanding which is limited to perceiving the discords, antinomies and contrasts
characterizing finite existence; he has risen to that
exalted state where all these find their resolution in
the blissful concord of the Eternal. He is in
conscious sympathy and identity of feeling with all
that lives and feels, in virtue of that universal
charity and limitless love which is the corollary of
perceiving the unity of all in the Being of Deity,
and which at the outset of his progress he was told
was the summit of the Mason's profession. He
sees too that there is a universe within as well as
without him; that he himself microcosmically sums
up and contains all that manifested to his temporal
intelligence as the vast spacial universe around him.
He is himself conscious of being the measure of
the universe; he realizes that the earth, the heavens,
and all their contents, are externalizations, projected
images, of corresponding realities present within
himself. As the perfected head of creation, he
beholds how he sums up in himself all the lower
forms of life through which his organism has passed
to attain to that perfection. The four symbolic
standards exhibiting the lion, ox, man and eagle
are a very ancient glyph, declaring among other

155

things the story of the soul's evolution and its
progress from the passional wild-beast stage to one
which, while still sensuous and animal, is docile
and disciplined for service, and thence to the stage
of human rationality, which at length culminates in
upward-soaring spirituality. Similarly the displayed
banners of the twelve Israelitish tribes are again
but figures of their prototypes, the twelve zodiacal
sections of those heavens which could not exist or
be discernible to the outward eye were they not also
the phenomenalized aspect of a reality cognizable
by the inward eye ; whilst, gathered beneath these
emblems, are those who represent the tribes of no
terrestrial nation, but are the " tribes of God," the
heavenly hierarchies that constitute an archetypal
canopy or holy royal arch above the visible creation
and that mediate to it the effluences of that all-
embracing triune Spirit of Power, Wisdom and
Love in which the entire composite structure lives,
moves and has its being.

" In the beginning God created the heavens and
the earth, and the earth was without form and void,
and darkness was upon the face of the deep. And
God said, Let there be light, and there was light."
With these words begins the Sacred Script which
is the sacramental token of that Living Word by
whom all things were made, and are still in the
making, and whose life is the light of men. The
candidate who recovers that lost Word, in the sense
of regaining vital organic integration into it, and
who, therefore, is one with its Life and its Light, is
able to verify this old creation-story in its personal
application to himself. He stands in the presence

of his own " earth "—the stone vault or dense matrix out of which his finer being has emerged— and of his own " heavens " or ethereal body of substantialized radiance which (as the iridescent sash of the Order is meant to denote) now covers him with light as with a garment. He is able to discern that it was himself who at first was " without form and void " and who in virtue of that *Fiat Lux !* has at last become transformed from chaos and unconsciousness into a form so perfect and lucid as to become a co-conscious vehicle of Divine Wisdom itself.

With this symbolic attainment of Beatific Vision at the restoration to light, the effective part of the Royal Arch Ceremony as an initiatory rite concludes. What follows upon it is anti-climax and allegorical exposition of a similar nature to the traditional history in the Master Mason's Degree. This takes the form of a mythos or dramatic narrative by the three sojourners, describing their release from captivity in Babylon, their return to Jerusalem under an impulse to assist in rebuilding the destroyed national temple, their work among its ruins and the discovery of an ancient and apparently important archive. The perspicacious mind will not fail to perceive in this historical or quasi-historical narrative an allegory of the spiritual process which has been going on within the candidate himself. It is he, as it is every human soul, that has been in Babylonian bondage, in captivity to the Babel-confusion of mundane existence, the tyranny of material interests, and the chaos of his own disordered nature. It is he who, in revolt from these, has in reflective

moments " sat down and wept by the waters of
Babylon "—the transient flux of temporal things—
and " remembered Zion," in a yearning for inward
freedom and permanent peace of heart. It is he
who finds the temple of his old natural self worthless
and in ruins, and realizes that upon its site he must
rebuild another and worthier one. From within
himself comes the urge of the inward Lord (*Kurios*)
which (under the mask of *Cyrus* the king) bids him
forthwith depart from his captivity and go up to
his true native-land and re-erect the Lord's house.
It is himself who discovers among the rubble of
his old self the plans and the material for the new
structure. And ultimately when that new structure
is completed and, when from natural man he has
become reorganized into spiritual man, it is he who
is able to perceive the wonders of his own constitution, to behold his own " earth " and his own
" heavens " now fused into a unity to which both
his material and his spiritual nature were necessary
contributors.

The constitution of the Chapter as first revealed
to the candidate is, therefore, a symbol of his
perfected organism. He sees that it is polarized
East and West; the East occupied by the three
Principals, signifying his spiritual pole; the West,
occupied by the three Sojourners, his psychic and
materialized pole; each triad being the reflex of
the other, yet each triad being an organic unity in
itself. St. John testifies to this (and the ceremonial
rite is made conformable to the teaching of that
great Initiate) when he writes : " There are three
that bear record in heaven, and these three are one.

And there are three that bear witness in earth, and these three agree in one." The meaning of this metaphysical assertion is that, just as a ray of white light splits up (as in the rainbow) into three primary colours which still remain organically united, so both the self-knowing Spirit in man and his psychical nature, although monadic essentially, are prismatically dissociable into a trinity. The Spirit in man in its triple aspects is, therefore, appropriately typified by the three Principals. They represent the three high attributes of the Spirit—Holiness, Royal Supremacy, Functional Power—referred to in the title of the Order; Holy-Royal-Arch. The middle and neutral term of these three must be considered as differentiating itself into a passive and an active, or a negative and a positive aspect; although all three act conjointly and as one (as is in fact the case with the three Principals of a Chapter). These three aspects of monadic Spirit are personified as Haggai (passive), Joshua (active), with Zerubabel as the middle term from which the other two issue and into which they merge. For the central Majesty is in one of its aspects silent and withdrawn and in the other functionally active and compulsive.

So too, with the triad of Sojourners at the other pole. They represent the unitary human Ego or personality also in its threefold aspects. They are the incarnated antitype or physicalized reflex of man's archetypal unincarnated and overshadowing Spirit. Hence they are designated Sojourners, as being but transient consociated pilgrims or wayfarers upon a plane of impermanence, in contrast with the enduring life of the deathless spirit whose

159

projection upon this lower world they are. Psychologically, human personality is distributed into a passive negative subconsciousness and an active positive intelligence, linked together by a central co-ordinating principle, the combined three constituting man's unitary individuality. My Ego with its central and directive power of will is my principal sojourner; my subconsciousness with its passive intuitional capacity, and my practical intelligence with its active and connecting powers of thought and understanding, are my assistant sojourners. Let me see to it that, like their symbolic representatives, they are kept clothed in white and so able to reflect and react to their correspondences in the eastern or spiritual pole of my being.

The nexus or connecting medium between man's spiritual and bodily poles is represented by a third triad impersonated by the two Scribes and the Janitor. The more important of these scribes is attached to the East pole and is as it were its emissary towards the West; the other is associated with the Western pole and his activities are directed Eastwards; whilst the Door-keeper is the point of contact with the world without. In one of their many significances they typify the middle term between Spirit and Matter—the astral medium or psychic bridge, in virtue of which contact between them is possible.

Heavily veiled beneath the sacramentalism of a council of the Jewish Sanhedrim, the Royal Arch Ceremony therefore exhibits in a most graphic manner the psychologic *rationale* of the final stage of regeneration. To the literalist, unacquainted

with the fact that, in both Sacred Writ and the
teaching of the Mysteries, surface appearances are
always intended to be transposed into spiritual
values and that quasi-historic characters are meant
to be impersonations of philosophic facts or principles, some difficulty may be felt on being asked to
translate the quasi-historicity of the ceremonial text
into the spiritualized interpretation here offered.
The education and enlightenment of the understanding is, however, one of the deliberate intentions
of Initiatory Rites, and until the mind is able to
rise above merely material facts and habituate itself
to functioning in the truer realm of ideas which
materialize into facts and make facts possible, there
is small chance of its profiting from Rites like those
of Masonry, which are of wholly negligible value
but for the spiritual force and vitalizing energy of
their inherent ideas. It may, therefore, be both
helpful and a corroboration of what has been said
if we scrutinize the Hebrew names of a Chapter's
officers ; what they yield upon analysis will demonstrate that those officers impersonate ideas rather
than represent persons.

1. " *Zerubabel, prince of the people.*" The name
literally means " a sprouting forth from Babel, or
from among the people." " Babel " and " people "
are two forms of expressing the same idea and the
English word is almost identical with the Hebrew
one. Society as a whole, the multitude, " the
people " (" *bebeloi*," as it is in Greek), at all times
of the world's history constitutes a Babel of confused
aims and interests. But there are always individuals
intellectually or spiritually in advance of the crowd

and whose ideas, teachings or example shoot ahead
of it, and to such leaders the name Zerubabel would
apply. But this illustration does not express the
deeper sense in which the word must be construed,
which is one of *personal* application. The individual
is himself a mob, a chaos, a multitude of confused
desires, thoughts, passions, until these are brought
into discipline. But, present even amidst these and
sprouting up from among them, the ordinary man
is conscious of a higher and spiritual element in
him, which he may cultivate or disregard, but which
in his best moments flames up above his lower
disordered nature, convinces him of the errors
of his ways, and entices him to live from that higher
level. That loftier element is expressed by the
word " Zerubabel " ; it is the apex and focus point
of his spirituality as distinguished from his ordinary
carnal intelligence ; the summit of all his faculties,
the " prince " of his " people." Those same
faculties or " people " are referred to in the word
meaning " My people having obtained mercy " (or
become regenerate), and in the text " The people
that sat in darkness have seen a great light."

2. " *Haggai the Prophet*." As has been shown
before, the spiritual principle differentiates into a
passive and an active aspect. " Haggai " represents
the passive aspect and signifies at once the blissful
and self-contemplative nature of the spirit. It is
called " the prophet " because of the power of
insight and omniscience characterizing that which
transcends the sense of time and abides eternally,
and because it projects into the lower intelligence
intuitions, foreglimpses and intimations of a

prophetic nature. From the same word is derived the Greek word " hagios," holy.

3. *" Joshua, the son of Josedek, the high priest,"* personifies the active executive aspect of spirit. Literally Joshua means the " divine saviour," and Josedek " divine righteousness," whilst the " high priest " connotes a mediatorial factor between man and Deity. The title in its entirety therefore intimates that the human spirit or divine principle in man functions intermediately between Deity and man's lower nature to promote the latter's salvation and perfection. We have previously shown how the Master Mason must be his own high priest and " walk upon " the chequered floor-work of his elementary nature by learning to trample upon it. Thus the Three Principals form a unity figuring man's spiritual pole in its triple aspects ; they represent the summit of his being as it lives on the plane of the Spirit—holy, royal, supreme—blissful because in a state of holiness or wholeness ; royal because a son of the King of all ; powerful because of its power to subdue, transmute and redeem all that is below its own purity and perfection.

4 & 5. *Ezra* and *Nehemiah.* In the great Mystery-system of Egypt, which long anteceded the Hebrew system, the regenerate candidate, who had achieved the highest possible measure of self-transmutation of his lower nature, was accorded the title of Osiris. It was the equivalent of attaining Christhood. The nature of the perfectioning process and the rituals in connection therewith are, thanks to certain modern scholars, available to us and are recommended to the student who desires to know how arduous and real

that process was and the extremely high degree of regeneration aimed at. In Hebrew the title Osiris became changed into Azarias (and sometimes Zeruiah) and still further corrupted into Esdras and Ezra, the name of the senior Scribe of the Royal Arch. To understand the significance of the two Scribes Ezra and Nehemiah it is necessary to recall that, in the Biblical account of the return from Babylonian captivity, these two were leading men. Transposing this historicized narrative into its spiritual implication, Ezra and Nehemiah personify two distinct stages of the mystical progress made by the candidate who essays to renounce the Babel of his lower nature and, by reorganizing himself, regain his native spiritual home and condition. " Nehemiah " (whose place in the Chapter is in the South West) is a figure of a certain measure of that reorganization and return. Like his Biblical proto-type, he symbolizes the candidate engaged in rebuilding the wall of Jerusalem, and occupied in the great work of self-reconstruction, from which he will not be beguiled into coming down by the appeals and blandishments of the outer world. " Ezra " (whose position is in the North East) indicates a much more advanced measure of progress from West to East. The discerning student who will peruse the Biblical books of Nehemiah and Ezra (including the Apocryphal books of Esdras) in this light, and with this key to their true purport, will not fail to profit by the instruction they will yield. Hence too they are called " scribes " ; both of them are recorders of, and testifiers to, distinct but representative experiences encountered in the inner man at different stages of the " great work " of self-integration and journeying from a Babylon condition to the spiritual Jerusalem.

Here we bring to an end our examination of the true meaning and purpose of the Royal Arch Ceremony. Dealing as it does with a supreme human experience which none can fully appreciate without undergoing it, it is the greatest and most momentous rite in Masonry, and no one who studies it comprehendingly and in its sacramental significance will withhold admiration either for the profound knowledge and insight of the now unidentifiable mystic and initiate who conceived it or for the skill with which he compiled it and cast his knowledge into dramatic expression. The pity of it is that those who practise the rite make no effort to penetrate its meaning and are content with the unenlightened perfunctory performance of a ritual which even exoterically is singularly striking, beautiful and suggestive. The least reflection upon it must suggest that Masonry is here dealing with the building-work of no outward structure, but with the re-erection of the fallen, disordered temple of the human soul ; and that even assuming that it but memorialized some long past historic events, those events can have no vital bearing upon the life, character or conduct of anyone to-day and would not justify the existence of an elaborate secret Order to perpetuate them. But if those events and this rite be symbolic of something deeper and something personal ; if they sacramentalize truths perpetually valid and capable of present realization in those who ceremonially re-enact them, then they call for fuller and more serious attention than is usually accorded. Moreover, if the Royal Arch be the symbolic representation of a supreme experience attained and attainable only in sanctity and by the regenerate, it follows that the Craft Degrees leading up to and qualifying for it will take on a much deeper sense than they commonly receive and must be regarded as solemn instructions in the requisite preparation for that regenerate condition. The Craft work is unfinished without the attainment forthshadowed in the Royal Arch. That attainment in turn is impossible without the discipline of the preliminary labours, the purification of mind and desire, and that crucifixion unto death of the self-will which constitute the tests of merit qualifying for entrance to that Jerusalem which has no geographical site and which is called the " City of Peace " because it implies conscious rest of the soul in God. For many, the suggestion that the attainment of such a condition is possible or thinkable whilst we are still here in the flesh may be surprising or even incredible. But such doubt is unwarranted, and the Masonic doctrine negates it. As has been already shown to the contrary, that doctrine postulates not the absence but the possession of the material organism as a necessary factor in advancing the evolution of the human spirit ; that organism is the vessel in which our base metal has to be transmuted into gold ; it is the fulcrum furnishing the resistance requisite for the spirit's energizing into unfoldment and self-consciousness. Physical death is therefore not an advancement of, but an interference with, the work of regeneration. " The night cometh when no man can work," and when the soul merely passes from labour to refreshment until recalled to labour once more at the task of self-conquest. It is but figurative of that necessary dying to self which implies the voluntary decreasing assertiveness of our temporal nature to permit of a corresponding ascendancy of the spiritual.

But if in the hands of its present exponents Masonry is now rather a dead letter than a living effectual Initiatory Rite capable of quickening the spirituality of its candidates, it still remains for the earnest and perspicuous aspirant to the deeper verities an instructive economy of the science of self-gnosis and regeneration. For such these papers are written, that they may both learn something of the original design of the Order and educate their imagination in the principles of that science. And to such, in conclusion, may be commended that Temple-hymn of the Hebrew Initiates, which of all the Psalms of David refers with most pointed reference to the subject-matter of the supreme Order of the Holy Royal Arch of Jerusalem and the personal attainment of the blessed and perfected condition which that title implies :—

> " I was glad when they said unto me, let us go up into
>   the house of the Lord ;
> Our feet shall stand within thy gates, O Jerusalem.
> Jerusalem is builded as a city that is compact together ;
> Thither the tribes go up, the tribes of the Lord....
> For there are set thrones of judgment, the thrones of
>   the house of David.
> Pray for the peace of Jerusalem ! they shall prosper
>   that love it.

Peace is within her walls and plenteousness within her
   palaces.
For my brethren and companions' sake I will say,
   Peace be within thee.   (*Psalm CXXII.*)

In those few lines is sketched all that is implied
in the symbolic spectacle that greets the eyes of the
Royal Arch Mason at the supreme moment of his
restoration to light. Exalted into and become
identified with the supreme bliss, peace and self-
consciousness of the All-Pervasive and Omniscient
Spirit, he sees how he has " gone up " out of the
Babylon of his old complex and disordered nature
and upon its ruins has built for himself an ethereal
body of glory, a " house of the Lord." He sees
how this ecstatic condition and this new-made
celestial body are the sublimated products of his
former self and its temporal organism. He sees
how each separate part and faculty of that old
nature, or as it were each of the zodiacal divisions
of his own microcosm, has contributed its purified
essence to form a new organism, " a new heaven
and a new earth " ; and how these essences, like
twelve diversified tribes, have assembled conver-
gently and finally coalesced and become fused into
a unity or new whole, " a city that is compact
together." And it is this " city," this blessed
condition, which mystically is called "Jerusalem,"
within whose walls is the peace which passeth
understanding and whose palaces reveal to the
enfranchised soul the unfailing plenteousness and
fecundity of the indissoluble trinity of Wisdom and
Love and Power from which man and the universe
have issued and into which they are destined to return.

The antithesis of this " heavenly city " is the confused Babylon city of this world, of which it is written to all captives therein, " Come out of her, My people, that ye be not partakers of her sins and that ye receive not of her plagues ! " (*Rev.* xviii. 4). And, in a word, the Royal Arch Ceremony sacramentally portrays the last phase of the mystical journey of the exiled soul from Babylon to Jerusalem as it escapes from its captivity to this lower world and, " passing the veils " of matter and form, breaks through the bondage of corruption into the world of the formless Spirit and realizes the glorious liberty of the children of God.

Chapter V.
FREEMASONRY IN RELATION TO
THE ANCIENT MYSTERIES.

EVERY Mason is naturally desirous to know something of the origin and history of the Craft. The available literature on the subject is diffuse and unsatisfying. It offers a mass of disconnected details of archæology and comparative religion without unifying them into any helpful light and deals rather with matters of minor and temporal history than with what alone is of real moment, the spiritual lineage of the Craft. In this paper, therefore, it is proposed to trace a rough outline—and, in the space available, only a very rough one is possible—of a movement which is as old as humanity itself and the purpose and doctrine of which are still faithfully, if very rudimentarily, preserved in the Masonic system. But such a sketch, by providing a general outline for the enquirer to contemplate and the details of which he may fill in for himself by subsequent study of his own, may perhaps prove more serviceable than a mass of fragmentary facts over which one may pore indefinitely and with much interest, yet without perceiving their inter-relation or co-ordinating them into one comprehensive impressive scheme.

No really serviceable work upon Masonry exists that treats of its history and purpose in the only way that matters vitally. The student is apt to waste much time to little profit by turning for information to publications the titles of which seem

to promise full enlightenment, but that leave him
unsatisfied and unconvinced. Desultory collections of
information upon points of symbolism, archæology
and anthropology, the tracing of connections between
modern Masonry and mediæval building-guilds and
other communities may be all very interesting, but
these are but as the dry bones of a subject of which
one desires to know the living spirit. They fail
to answer the main questions one asks from the
heart and is anxious to have answered; such as,
What was the nature of the Ancient Mysteries of
which modern Masonry purports to be the perpetuation? To what end and purpose did they exist?
What need is there to perpetuate them to-day?
For what purpose was Initiation instituted? Did
it at any time serve any real purpose or can it now?
Was it ever more than it is to-day, a mere perfunctory
ceremonial leading to nothing of essential value and
emphasizing only a few moral principles and
elementary truths which we know already? It is
to answering such questions as these that the
present paper is directed.

Now one of the first things to strike any student
of Masonic literature and comparative religion is
the remarkable presence of common factors, common
beliefs, doctrines, practices and symbols, in the
religions of all races alike, whether ancient or modern,
eastern or western, civilized or barbarian, Christian
or pagan. However separated from others by time
or distance, however intellectualized or primitive,
however elaborated or simple their religion or
morals, and however wide their differences in
important respects, each people is found to have

employed and still to be employing certain ideas,
symbols and practices in common with every other ;
perhaps with or without some slight modification
of form. Masonic treatises abound with demon-
strations of this uniformity in the use of various
symbols prominent in every Lodge. Authors delight
in supplying evidence of the close correspondences
in various unrelated systems and in demonstrating
how ancient and universal such and such ideas,
symbols and practices have been. But they do not
go so far as to explain the reason for this antiquity
and universality, and it is this point which it will
be well to clear up at the outset, since it furnishes
the clue to the entire problem of the genesis, the
history, and the reason for the existence of Masonry.

If research and reflection be pushed far enough
it becomes clear that the universality and uniformity
referred to are due to the fact that at one time,
long back in the world's past, there existed or was
implanted in the minds of the whole human family—
which was doubtless much smaller and more
concentrated then than now—a Proto-Evangelium
or Root-Doctrine in regard to the nature and
destiny of the soul of man and its relation to the
Deity. We of to-day pride ourselves upon being
wiser and more advanced than primitive humanity.
We assume that our ancestors lived in moral
benightedness out of which we have since gradually
emerged into comparative light. All the evidence,
however, negatives these suppositions. It indicates
that primitive man, however childish and intellectually undeveloped according to modern standards,
was spiritually conscious and psychically perceptive

to a degree undreamed of by the modern mind, and that it is ourselves who, for all our cleverness and intellectual development in temporal matters, are nevertheless plunged in darkness and ignorance about our own nature, the invisible world around us, and the eternal spiritual verities. In all Scriptures and cosmologies the tradition is universal of a " Golden Age," an age of comparative innocence, wisdom and spirituality, in which racial unity and individual happiness and enlightenment prevailed ; in which there was that open vision for want of which a people perisheth, but in virtue of which men were once in conscious conversation with the unseen world and were shepherded, taught and guided by the " gods " or discarnate superintendents of the infant race, who imparted to them the sure and indefeasible principles upon which their spiritual welfare and evolution depended.

The tradition is also universal of the collective soul of the human race having sustained a " fall," a moral declension from its true path of life and evolution, which has severed it almost entirely from its creative source, and which, as the ages advanced, has involved its sinking more and more deeply into physical conditions, its splitting up from a unity employing a single language into a diversity of conflicting races of different speeches and degrees of moral advancement, accompanied by a progressive densification of the material body and a corresponding darkening of the mind and atrophy of the spiritual consciousness. To some who read this the statement will probably be rejected as fabulous and incredible. The supposition of a

" fall of man " is nowadays an unpopular doctrine, rejected by many who contend that everything points rather to a rise of man, yet who fail to reflect that logically a rise necessarily involves an antecedent fall from which a rise becomes possible. This point, however, we cannot stop to discuss and must be content merely with indicating what in both the Scriptures of all races and the Wisdom-tradition of the sages of antiquity is unanimously recorded to be the fact.

From that " fall," which was not due to the transgression of an individual, but to some weakness or defect in the collective or group-soul of the Adamic race, and which was not the matter of a moment but a process covering vast time-cycles, it was necessary and within the Divine counsels and providence that humanity should be redeemed and restored to its pristine state ; that it should be brought back once more into vital association with the Divine Principle from which by its secession it became increasingly detached, as its materialistic tendencies overpowered and quenched its native spirituality. This restoration in turn required vast time-cycles for its achievement. And it required something further. It required the application of an orderly and scientific method to effect the restoration of each fallen soul-fragment and bring it back to its primitive pure and perfect condition. I emphasize that the method was necessarily to be not a haphazard, but a scientific one. Anyone may fall from a housetop and break his bones ; skilled surgery and intelligent effort by some friendly hand are required to heal the patient and get him back to the place he fell from. So with humanity. It fell—out of Eden, as our Scriptures describe the lapse from super-physical to physical conditions—why and how, again we must not stay to enquire. It fell, through inherent weakness and lack of wisdom. Unable to effect its own recovery it required skilled scientific assistance from other sources to bring about its restoration. Whence could come that skill and scientific knowledge if not from the Divine and now invisible world, from those " gods " and angelic guardians of the erring race of whom all the ancient traditions and sacred writings tell? Would not that regenerative method be properly described if it were called, as in Masonry it *is* called, a " heavenly science," and welcomed in the words that Masons in fact use, " Hail, Royal Art ! " ?

Thus, then, was the origin and birth of Religion. And Religion is a word implying a " binding back " (*re-ligare*). As with the setting and bandaging a broken limb, so the collective soul of humanity, fractured and comminuted by its fall into countless individuations and their subsequent respective progenies, each separately damaged and imperfect, needed to be restored to the condition from which it had become dislocated and once more built up into a perfect harmonious whole.

To the spiritual guardians of primitive man, then, one must attribute the communication of that universal science of rebuilding the fallen temple of humanity, of which science we now surprisedly find traces in every race and religion of the world. To this source we must credit the distribution, in every land and among every people, of the same or

equivalent symbols, practices and doctrines, modified only locally and in accordance with the
intelligence of particular peoples, yet all manifesting
a common root and purpose.

This was the one Holy Catholic (or universal)
Religion " throughout all the world " ; at once a
theoretic doctrine and a practical science intended
to reunite man to his Maker. That religion could
only be one, as it could not be otherwise than
catholic and for all men equally and alike; though,
owing to the perverse distortive tendencies of
humanity itself, it was susceptible of becoming (as
has so happened) debased and sectarianized into as
many forms as there are peoples. Moreover, its
main principles could never be susceptible of
alteration, though they might be (as they have been)
exoterically understood by some and esoterically by
others, and their full import would not all at once
be apparent, but develop with increasing fidelity to
and understanding of them. It provided the
unalterable " landmarks " of knowledge concerning
human nature, human potentialities and human
destiny. It laid down the ancient and established
"usages and customs" to be followed at all times by
everyone content to accept its discipline and which
none might deviate from or add innovations to, save
at his own peril. It was the " Sacred Law " for the
guidance of the fallen soul, a law valid from the dawn
of time till its sunset, and of which it is written "As
it was in the beginning, is now and ever shall be,
world without end." It was the science of life—of
temporal limited life lived with the intention of its
conversion and sublimation into eternal universal

life; and, therefore, it called for a scientific or philosophic method of living, every moment and action of which should be directed to that great goal;—a method very different from the modern method, which is entirely utilitarian in its outlook and totally unscientific in its conduct.

This Proto-Religion is related to have originated in the East, from which proverbially all light comes, and, as humanity itself became diffused and distributed over the globe, to have gradually spread towards the West, in a perpetual watchfulness of humanity's spiritual interests and an unfailing purpose to retrieve " that which was lost "—the fallen human soul. We have already said that in early times the humanity then under its influence was far less materialized and far more spiritually sensitive and perceptive than it subsequently became or is now; and accordingly it follows that with the increasing age and density of the race the influence of the Proto-Religion itself became correspondingly diminished, though its principles remained as valid and effective as before; for the self-willed vagaries and speculative conceptions of man cannot alter the principles of static Truth and Wisdom. To follow in any detail the course of its history is not now necessary and would require a long treatise. And to do so would also be like following the course of a river backwards from its broad mouth to a point where it becomes an insignificant and scarcely traceable channel. For the race itself has wandered backwards, farther and farther from the original Wisdom-teaching, so that the once broad and bright flood of light upon cosmic principles and the

evolution of the human soul has now become
contracted into minute points. But that light, like
that of a Master Mason, has never been wholly
extinguished, however dark the age, and, by the
tradition, this of ours is spiritually the darkest of
the dark ages. " God has never left Himself
without a witness among the children of men,"
and among the witnesses to the Ancient Wisdom
and Mysteries is the system of Masonry ; a faint
and feeble flicker, perhaps, but nevertheless a true
light and in the true line of succession of the primitive doctrine, and one still able to guide our feet into
the way of peace and perfection.

The earliest teaching of the Mysteries traceable
within historic time was in the Orient and in the
language known as Sanscrit—a name itself significant
and appropriate, for it means Holy Writ or " *Sanctum
Scriptum* " ; and for very great lights upon the
ancient Secret Doctrine one must still refer to the
religious and philosophical scriptures of India,
which was in its spiritual and temporal prime when
modern Europe was frozen beneath an ice-cap.

But races, like men, have their infancy, manhood
and old age ; they are but units, upon a larger scale
than the individual, for furthering the general
life-purpose. When a given race has served or
failed in that purpose, the stewardship of the
Mysteries passes on to other and more effectual
hands. The next great torch-bearer of the Light
of the world was Egypt, which, after many centuries
of spiritual supremacy, in turn became the arid
desert it now is both spiritually and materially,
leaving nevertheless a mass of structural and written

relics still testifying to its possession of the Doctrine in the days of its glory. From Egypt, as civilizations developed in adjoining countries, a great irradiation of them took place by the diffusion of its knowledge and the institution of minor centres for the imparting of the Divine Science in Chaldea, Persia, Greece and Asia Minor. " Out of Egypt have I called My son " is, in one of its many senses, a biblical allusion to this passing on of the catholic Mysteries from Egypt to new and virgin regions, for their enlightenment.

Of these various translations those that concern us chiefly are two ; the one to Greece, the other to Palestine. We know from the Bible that Moses was an initiate of the Egyptian mysteries and became learned in all its wisdom, while Philo tells us that Moses there became " skilled in music, geometry, arithmetic, hieroglyphics and the whole circle of arts and sciences." In other words he became in a real sense a Master Mason and, as such, qualified himself for his subsequent great task of leadership of the Hebrew people and the formulating of their religious system and rule of life as laid down in the Pentateuch. The Mosaic system continued, as we know, along the channel indicated in the books of the Old Testament, and then, after many centuries and vicissitudes, effloresced in the greatest of all expressions of the Mysteries, as disclosed in the Gospels of the New Testament (or New Witness), involving the super-session of all previous systems under the Supreme Grand Mastership of Him who is called the Light of the World and its Saviour.

Concurrently with the existence of the Hebrew

Mysteries under the Mosiac dispensation, the great
Greek school of the Mysteries was developing,
which, originating in the Orphic religion, culminated
and came to a focus at Delphi and generated the
philosophic wisdom and the æsthetic glories
associated with Athens and the Periclean age. Greece
was the spiritual descendant and infant prodigy of
both India and Egypt, though developing along quite
different lines. We know that Pythagoras, like Moses,
after absorbing all his native teachers could impart,
journeyed to Egypt to take his final initiation prior
to returning and founding the great school at
Crotona associated with his name. We know, too,
from the *Timæus* of Plato how aspirants for mystical
wisdom visited Egypt for initiation and were told
by the priests of Sais that " you Greeks are but
children " in the Secret Doctrine, but were admitted
to information enabling them to promote their own
spiritual advancement. We know from the correspondence, recorded by Iamblichus, between Anebo
and Porphyry, the fraternal relations existing between
the various schools or lodges of instruction in
different lands ; how their members visited, greeted
and assisted one another in the secret science, the
more advanced being obliged, as every initiate still is
when called upon, to " afford assistance and instruction to his brethren in the inferior degrees." And
we know that at the Nativity—or shall we say the
installation in this world—of the Great Master,
there came to Him from afar Magi or initiate-
visitors who knew of His impending advent and
had seen His star in the East and desired to acknow-
ledge and pay Him reverence. In all these world-

moving incidents in times when initiation was a real event and not a mere ceremonial form as now, it is of interest to notice the practice upon a grand scale of the same customs and courtesies as are still observed, though alas unintelligently, by the Craft of to-day.

We must now speak more fully of the Mysteries and the " Royal Art " as pursued by the Greek school. With the Greeks it took the form of a quest of philosophy; *i.e.*, for wisdom, for the Sophia, just as in the Hebrew and Christian schools it took the form of a quest for the Lost Word. The end was of course the same in both cases, but the approach to it was by different means and, as we shall see, the two methods coalesced into one at a later date. The Greek approach was primarily an intellectual one and by what Spinoza has termed *Amor intellectualis Dei*. The Christian approach was primarily through the affections and the adoration of the heart. Both strained after " that which was lost," but one sought after the lost ideal by intellectual and the other by devotional energy. Humanity is but slowly educated; " line upon line; precept upon precept; here a little and there a little," one faculty after another being developed and trained unto the refashioning of the perfect organism. And if philosophic Wisdom and the sense of Beauty stood forth—as they did stand forth—most prominently as the main pillars of the Greek system, the Greeks had yet to learn of a third and middle pillar that synthesized and comprised them both—that of the Strength of the supreme virtue of Love, when towards the object

181

of all desire it pours from a pure and perfect heart.

The Greek's quest of wisdom was something much more than a mere desire for larger information and maturer judgment about one's place in the universe. Merely to know certain facts about the hidden side of life profits nothing unless the knowledge is allowed to influence and adapt our method of living to the truths disclosed. Then the knowledge becomes transmuted into wisdom; one *becomes* the truth one sees; and a man's life becomes truth made substantial and dynamic. But to bring this about one must first be informed about or initiated into certain elements of the truth and be persuaded that it *is* truth before setting about to become it. The Greek method, therefore, began by initiating the mind into certain truths about the soul's own nature, history, destiny and potentialities, and then left the individual to follow up the information by a course of conduct in which the teaching imparted would become converted into assured conviction and living power, whilst his increasing progress in the science would itself result in awakening him to still deeper truths.

It cannot be too strongly emphasized that no one can learn spiritual science, whether as taught by Masonry or any other system inculcating it, without submitting himself to its processes and living them out in practical experience. In this supreme study, knowing depends entirely upon doing; comprehension is conditional upon and the corollary of action. " He that will *do* the will shall *know* of the doctrine."

Hence it is that in Masonry an installed Master is still called a " *Master* of Arts and Sciences," for he is supposed to have mastered the art of living in accordance with the theoretic gnosis or science imparted to him in the course of his progress. Real Masonic knowledge will never be achieved merely by oral explanation, hearing lectures and studying books. These may be useful in giving a preliminary start to earnest seekers needing but a little guidance to set them on that path of personal practice and experience where they will soon develop an automatic understanding of the doctrine for themselves ; for those with but a casual dilletante interest the doctrine will continue veiled and secret. For example, it is one thing to hear explained what is meant by being divested of money and metals in the philosophic sense ; it is quite another to have become insusceptible to all attraction by material interests and sense-allurements and to be consciously possessed of the wisdom accruing from that experience. It may interest to be told why, at a certain stage of progress, the candidate is likened to an ear of corn by a fall of water ; but the explanation will be forgotten to-morrow, unless as the result of his own effort the hearer has become personally aware of an inward substantial growth ripening to harvest within him from the ground of his own being and fertilized by supersensual nourishment falling like the gentle rain from heaven upon his ardent and aspiring soul. Again, it may seem instructive to know that the great ritual of the Third Degree signifies a death unto sin and self and a new birth unto righteousness, but how will the information

profit those who nevertheless mean to go on
living the old manner of life, which at every
moment negates all that that ritual implies?

The Ancient Mysteries, then, involved much
more than a merely notional philosophy. They
required also a philosophic method of living—or
rather of dying. For as Socrates said (in Plato's
Phædo, from which much Masonic teaching is
directly drawn and which every Masonic student
should study deeply) " the whole study of the
philosopher (or wisdom-seeker) is nothing else than
to die and be dead "; an assertion repeated by
Plutarch, " to be initiated is to die "; and by the
Christian apostle, " I die daily." Their method
was divided into two parts, the Lesser and the
Greater Mysteries. The Lesser were those in which
the more elementary instruction was imparted, so
that candidates might forthwith set about to purify
and adapt their lives to the truths disclosed. The
Greater Mysteries related to the developments of
consciousness within the soul itself, as the result
of fidelity to the prescribed rule of life. To draw
a faint analogy, the Lesser Mysteries bore the same
relation to the Greater as the present Craft Degrees
do to the Holy Royal Arch.

To deal adequately with the Mystery-systems
would involve a lengthy study in itself. We will
refer to but one of the most famous of them, the
Eleusinian, which existed in Greece and for several
centuries was the focus-point of religion and
philosophy for the then civilized portion of Europe.
" Eleusis " means light, and initiation into the
Mysteries of Eleusis, therefore, meant a quest of

the aspirant for light, in precisely the same, but a far more real, sense as the modern Mason declares light to be the predominant wish of his heart. It meant, as it ought to mean to-day but does not, not merely light in the sense of being given some secret information not obtainable elsewhere or about any matter of worldly interest, but the opening up of the candidate's whole intellectual and spiritual nature in the super-sensual light of the Divine world and raising him to God-consciousness. The ordinary and uninitiated man knows nothing of that super-sensual light by his merely natural reason; he is conscious only of the outer world and things perceptible by his natural faculties. In the words of St. Paul " the natural man receiveth not the things of the Spirit of God, for they are foolishness unto him ; neither can he know them, because they are spiritually discerned." Initiation, therefore, meant a process whereby natural man became transformed into spiritual or ultra-natural man, and to effect this it was necessary to *change his consciousness*, to gear it to a new and higher principle, and so, as it were, make of him a new man in the sense of attaining a new method of life and a new outlook upon the universe. " Be ye transformed by the renewing of your minds," says the Apostle, referring to this process. As has previously been shown in these papers, the transference of the symbol of the Divine Presence from the ceiling to the floor of the Masonic Lodge is to indicate how the Vital and Immortal Principle in man can be brought down from his remoter psychological region into his physical organism and function there through his

185

body and brain, thus as it were dislocating and superseding his natural mentality and regenerating him. This truth is still further reproduced in Masonry by the name "Lewis," traditionally associated with the Craft. "Lewis" is a modern corruption of Eleusis and of other Greek and Latin names associated with Light. In our instruction Lectures it is said to designate " the son of a Mason." This, however, has no reference to human parentage and sonship. It refers to the mystical birth of the Divine Light in oneself; as a familiar Scriptural text has it, " Unto us a child is born, unto us a son is given." It is the Divine Principle, the Divine Wisdom, brought to birth and function within the organism of the natural man, who virtually becomes its parent. It is further described in our Lectures as something " which when properly dovetailed into a stone forms a clamp, enabling Masons to lift great weights with little inconvenience whilst fixing them on their proper bases." All which is a concealed way of expressing the fact that, when the Divine Light is brought forward from man's submerged depths and firmly grafted or dovetailed into his natural organism, he then becomes able easily to grapple with difficulties, problems and " weights " of all kinds which to the unregenerate are insuperable, and to perceive all things *sub specie æternitatis* and in their true relations, as is not possible to other men who behold them only *sub specie temporis* and are consequently unable to judge their real values and " fix them on their proper bases."

In the time that the Mysteries flourished, every

educated man entered them in the same way that
men enter a University in modern times. They
were the recognized source of instruction in the
only things that really matter, those affecting the
culture of the human soul and its education in the
science of itself and its divine nature. Candidates
were graded according to their moral efficiency
and their intellectual or spiritual stature. For years
they underwent disciplinary intellectual exercises
and bodily asceticism, punctuated at intervals by
appropriate tests and ordeals to determine their
fitness to proceed to the more serious, solemn and
awful processes of actual initiation, administered only
to the duly qualified, and which were of a secret and
closely   guarded   character.   Their   education,
differing greatly from the scholastic methods of a
utilitarian age like our own, was directed solely to
the cultivation of the " four cardinal virtues " and
the " seven liberal arts and sciences " as qualifications prerequisite to participation in the higher order
of life to which initiation would eventually admit
the worthy and properly prepared candidate. The
construction put upon these virtues and sciences
was a much more advanced one than the modern
mind considers adequate. Virtues with them were
more than abstractions and ethical sentiments; as the
word itself implies they involved positive valours and
virility of soul.   Temperance involved complete
control of the passional nature under every circumstance ; Fortitude, the courage that no adversity
will dismay or deflect from the goal in view ;
Prudence, the deep insight that begets the prophetic
or forward-seeing faculty of seer-ship (*providentia*);

*Free-
masonry
in
Relation
to the
Ancient
Mysteries*

Justice, unswerving righteousness of thought and
action.* The " arts and sciences " were called
" liberal " because they tended to *liberate* the soul
from defects and illusions normally enslaving it,
thus totally differing from science in the modern
sense, the tendency of which is, as we know,
materialistic and soul-benumbing. Grammar, Logic
and Rhetoric with the Ancients were disciplines of
the moral nature, by which the irrational tendencies
of a human being were purged away and he was
trained to become a living witness of the universal
Logos and a living mouth-piece of the Divine Word.
Geometry and Arithmetic were sciences of transcendental space and numeration (seeing that, as in
the words of our own Scriptures, God has " made
everything by measure, number and weight "), the
comprehension of which provides the key, not only
to the problems of one's being, but to those physical
ones which are found so baffling by the inductive
methods of to-day. Astronomy for them required
no telescopes ; it dealt not with the stars of the
sky, but was the science of metaphysics and the
understanding of the distribution of the forces latent
in, and determining the destiny of, individuals,
nations and the race. Finally Music (or Harmony)
was for them not of the vocal or instrumental kind ;
it meant the living practice of philosophy, the
adjustment of human life into harmony with God,
until the personal soul became unified with Him
and consciously heard, because it now participated

---

* The four cardinal virtues are referred to in both Plato's
Phædo and the *Book of Wisdom*, ch. viii, 5-7, indicating community of teaching between the Greek and Hebrew schools.

in, the music of the spheres. As Milton puts it :—

" How lovely is Divine Philosophy,
   Not harsh and crabbèd as dull fools suppose,
   But musical as is Apollo's lute
   And a perpetual feast of nectar'd sweets
   Where no crude surfeit reigns."

Every possible device was employed and practised to train the mind to acquire dominion over the passions and to loosen and detach it from the impressions and attractions of the senses, to destroy the illusions and false imaginations under which it labours when using no higher light than its own, and to qualify it for a higher method of cognition and for the reception of supersensual truth and the light of the Divine world. The idealism of Greek architecture and sculpture was entirely due to the same motive and with a view to elevating the imagination beyond the visible level and fitting the mind for the apprehension of ultra-physical form and beauty. Even athletic exercises were made to subserve the same purpose ; wrestling and racing were not vulgar sports ; they were regarded sacramentally, as the type of combats the soul must engage in against the competition of the fleshly desires ; and the victor's crown of laurel or olive was the emblem of wisdom and illumination resulting to him in whom the spirit conquers the flesh. Thus every intellectual and physical interest was made subservient to the one idea of separating the soul from material bondage and was purposely of a purifying or " cathartic " nature that should cleanse the thoughts and desires of the aspirant and make him white within and without even as the modern candidate for the

189

Craft is clothed in white. This inward purity of heart and mind, coupled with the possession of the four cardinal virtues, was and still is an absolute essential to the ordeals of actual initiation, which otherwise rendered the candidate liable to insanity and obsessions of which the modern mind in its ignorance of what initiation involves can form no opinion. Those who became proficient and properly prepared in this curriculum of the Lesser Mysteries were eventually admitted to initiation in the Greater Mysteries. Those who failed to qualify were restrained from advancement. As now, the numbers of really earnest and qualified aspirants were only a percentage of the total of those who entered the Mysteries, for in the spiritual life, as in the world of nature, the biological phenomenon prevails that the available raw material greatly exceeds the perfected product. Every year far more seeds are borne, far more eggs are laid or spawned, than reach maturity, although every seed and egg is potentially capable of growth and fruition. Plato, speaking of the Mysteries in his own day, quotes a still older authority that " the thyrsus-bearers* (or candidates for initiation) are numerous, but the Bacchuses (or perfected initiates) are few." The same truth is restated in the words in the Gospels, " Many are called, but few are chosen."

One qualification above all was essential to the

---

* The thyrsus (or *Caduceus*) was an elaborate wand borne by the candidate, to the symbolism of which deep meaning attached. Its present form is the wand carried by the deacon accompanying the candidate.

aspirant, as it is still to-day,—humility. The wisdom
into which the Mysteries and initiation admit a man
is foolishness to the world ; it is a reversal and
revolution of all orthodox and academic standards.
To attain it a man must be prepared for that complete
and voluntary self-denial which may involve his
finding negated everything he has previously held
to be true, or which those among whom he ordinarily
mingles believe to be true. He must be content
to " become a fool for the kingdom of heaven's sake "
and to suffer adversity, ridicule and obloquy for it if
needs be. This was one of the prime reasons for
secrecy and one—though not the only one—of the
origins of the Masonic injunction as to secrecy.
The world's wisdom and that to which initiation
admits are so antipodal in their nature that any
intrusion of the latter will infallibly provoke resent-
ment from the former. Hence it is written " Cast
not your pearls before swine, neither give that which
is holy unto dogs—*lest they turn and rend you.*"
Silence and secrecy are, therefore, desirable if only
in self-defence, though there are other reasons; but
humility is indispensable. In the public processions
of the Lesser Mysteries—for the public were
permitted at certain festivals to participate to a
small extent in some of the more exoteric knowledge
—the sacred emblems and eucharistic vessels used
in the rites were carried with great reverence upon
the back of an ass. With the same intention, it is
said that one of the great Greek philosophers always
had an ass by his side in his lecture-room when
instructing his students. The explanation is given
in the words of one of the old authorities upon

*Free-
masonry
in
Relation
to the
Ancient
Mysteries*

initiation as follows : " There is no creature so able to receive divinity as an ass, into whom if ye be not turned, ye shall in no wise be able to carry the divine mysteries." In the light of this, one will at once discern the symbolical significance of the Christian Master riding into Jerusalem upon an ass.

Another and a greatly educative means employed in the Mysteries was that of instructing, enlarging and purifying the imagination by means of myths, expressing either in doctrinal form or by spectacular representation, truths of the Divine world and of the soul's history. The modern mind in its passion for actual concrete facts is little sympathetic to a method of teaching which dispenses with demonstrable facts and prefers to enunciate the eternal principles underlying such facts and of which those facts are but the manifested resultant consequence. Facts—of history or science—tend, however, to congest the mind and paralyse the imagination, as Darwin lamented in his own case. Principles stimulate and illumine the imagination, and enable the mind to interpret facts and adjust them to their proper relation. The Greek mythologists were adepts at expressing cosmic and philosophic truths in the guise of fables which at once expressed theosophic teaching to the discerning and veiled it from the careless and ignorant. Myth-making was a science, not an indulgence in irresponsible fiction, and by exhibiting some of these myths in dramatic form candidates were instructed in various fundamental verities of life.

One of the chief and best known of the numerous

myths was that of Demeter and her daughter
Persephone, annually performed with great ceremony
and elaboration at the Eleusinia, and of which it
may be useful to speak briefly. It told how the
maiden Persephone strayed away from Arcadia
(heaven) and her mother Demeter, to pluck flowers
in the meads of Enna, and how the soil there opened
and caused her to fall through into the lower dark
world of Hades ruled over by Pluto. The despair
of her mother at the loss reached Zeus, the chief
of the Gods, with the result that he relieved the
position by ordaining that, if the girl had not eaten
of the fruit of Hades, she should forthwith be
restored to her mother for ever, but that if she had
so eaten she must abide a third of each year with
Pluto and return to Demeter for the other two
thirds. It proved that Persephone had unfortunately
eaten a pomegranate in the lower world, so that her
restoration to her mother could not be permanent,
but only periodic.

This myth, and the importance once attached to
it, will be appreciated only upon understanding its
interpretation. It is the story of the soul and is
of the same nature as the Mosaic myth of Adam
and Eve and the apple, and as the cosmic parable
of the Prodigal Son, neither of these being meant to
be regarded as historically true, but as a fiction
spiritually true of cosmic facts. Persephone is the
human soul, generated out of that primordial
incorruptible mother-earth which the Greeks
personified as Demeter, just as the Mosaic narrative
speaks of God forming man out of the dust of the
ground. Her straying from her Arcadian home

and heavenly mother in quest of flowers (or fresh experiences on her own account) in the fields of Enna, corresponds with the same promptings of desire that led to Adam's disobedience in Eden and his fall thence to this outer world. All unruly desires end in dissatisfaction and bitterness, and " Enna " (signifying darkness and bitterness) is the same word as still meets us in Gehenna. One may, however, profit by one's mistakes. It is they which breed wisdom, and it is the riches of wisdom and experience that are signified by Pluto, the god of riches, into whose kingdom Persephone falls. She might have returned thence to her mother for ever, Zeus decreed, had she not still further injured herself by eating of the fruit of the lower world, but having done so her restoration can only be partial and temporary. This alludes to the soul's still further self-soilure and degradation by lusting after the inferior pleasures of this lower plane, which, as the pomegranate symbolizes, is many-seeded with illusions and vanities. Until these false tendencies are eradicated, until the desires of the heart are utterly weaned from external delights, there can be no permanent restoration of the soul to its source, but merely the periodic respite and refreshment that death brings when it withdraws the soul from Pluto's realm to the heaven-world, to be followed again and again by periodic descents into material limitations and reascents into discarnate conditions, until it becomes finally purged and perfected.

By this great myth, therefore, instruction was imparted as to the history of the soul, its destiny

and prospects, and the doctrine of reincarnation*
was emphasized.

Now Masonry follows this traditional method of instruction by myths. Its canon of teaching in the Craft degrees contains two myths. One is that of the building of King Solomon's Temple. The other is that of the death and burial of Hiram Abiff narrated in the traditional history. The Royal Arch contains a third myth in the story of the return from captivity after the destruction of the first temple, the commencement to build the second, and the discovery then made. This third myth has already been expounded in our paper on the Royal Arch degree, so that we need now speak only of the Craft Myths.

To the literal-minded the building of Solomon's temple at Jerusalem (which is of course largely but not entirely based upon the Hebrew Scriptures) appears to be the history of an actual stone and mortar structure erected by three Asiatic notables, one of whom conceived the idea, another supplying the building material, whilst the third was the practical architect and chief of works. The two former are said to have been kings of adjacent small nations; the third was not a royalty, but apparently a person of no social dignity and a " widow's son."

As has previously been said in these papers, these details of an enterprise undertaken more than two

---

* As this doctrine is not popularly inculcated in the West as it is in the East, and will be novel and probably unacceptable to some readers, its acceptance is not pressed here. We are merely recording what the secret doctrine teaches.

thousand years ago can have no possible value to anyone to-day and if they related merely to historic fact modern Masonry might as well close its doors and cease to exist for any benefit that fact could impart to serious or reflective minds.   But if the narrative were never intended as a record of temporal historic fact, but be a myth enshrining philosophic truths concerning eternal principles, then it must be interpreted with spiritual discernment and its analysis will reveal matters of real importance.

The story of the building of the temple, then, is a philosophical instruction, garbed in quasi-historical form, concerning the structure of the human soul. That temple is not one of common brick and stone, but of the " unhewn stone " or incorruptible raw material of which the Creator fashioned the human organism.   The Jerusalem in which it was built was not the geographical one in Palestine, but the eternal " city of peace " in the heavens ; not, as St. Paul says, " the Jerusalem which now is, but the Jerusalem above, which is the mother of us all," like the Greek Demeter. Its builders were not three human personages resident in the Levant, but the Divine energy considered in its three constituent principles spoken of in our Instruction Lectures as Wisdom, Strength and Beauty, which as " pillars of His work " run through and form the metaphysical warp and basis of all created things. These three metaphysical principles may be defined in modern terms as Life-Essence (or the substantial spirit of Wisdom); incorruptible Matter, serving as the mould, matrix or vehicle of that Life-Essence, to give it fixity, form and objectiveness (Strength);

and lastly the fabricative intellectual principle or Logos binding these two together and constituting the whole an intelligent and functionally effective instrument (Beauty). Of these three principles, or upon these three pillars, was the human soul originally and divinely built in the heaven-world, and our Lectures, therefore, rightly say that those three pillars " also allude to Solomon, King of Israel ; Hiram, King of Tyre ; and Hiram Abiff," because those names personify the indissociable triadic constituents of the Divine Unity. (They are also shown inscribed upon the central symbolic altar in the Royal Arch Degree as further evidence of this divine construction of the human soul). The temple of the soul has, however, now been destroyed and thrown down from its primitive eminence and grandeur. Humanity, instead of being a collective united organic whole, has become shattered into innumerable fragmentary separated parts, not one stone standing upon another of its ruined building. It has lost consciousness of the genuine secrets of its own origin and nature and has now to be content with the spurious substituted knowledge it picks up from sense-impressions in this outer world. Like Persephone it has eaten the pomegranates of Pluto's dark realm in preference to the ambrosia of Arcady, and until that poison is eliminated from its system it cannot permanently reattain its unfallen state, but at best must endure a rhythm of deaths and rebirths and of intermittent periods of labour in this world and refreshment beyond it. But it may become cleansed ; the temple can be rebuilt, and each Mason's soul that is wrought into a true die or

square by his work upon himself here, becomes one
more new stone of the restored temple in the
heavens.

A further word is necessary as to the concealed
significance of Solomon and the two Hirams.
Solomon personifies the primordial Life-Essence
or substantialized Divine Wisdom which is the basis
of our being. It is defined in the *Book of Wisdom*
(chap. vii., 25-27), as "a pure influence flowing
from the glory of the Almighty; the brightness of
the everlasting light, the unspotted mirror of the
power of God and the image of His goodness."
It is described as a "king" because it must needs
transcend and over-rule whatever is inferior to
itself, and as "king of Israel" because "Israel"
itself means "co-operating or ruling with God"
as distinct from being associated with beings or
affairs of a sub-divine order. To conjoin this
transcendental Life-Essence to a vehicle which
should give it fixity and form required the assistance
of another dominant or "kingly" principle, personified as Hiram, King of Tyre, who supplied the
"building material." Now inasmuch as we are
dealing with purely metaphysical ideas, it will be
obvious that the Tyre in question has no relation
to the Levantine sea-port of that name. The name
Tyre in Hebrew means "rock" and the strength,
compactness and durability which we associate with
rock, whilst the same word recurs in Greek as *Turos*
and in Latin as *Terra*, earth, and as *Durus*, implying
form, hardness, consistency and durability. "King
of Tyre," therefore, is interpretable as the cosmic
principle which gives solidity and form to the

spiritual fluidic and formless Life-Essence, and which is comparable to a cup intended to hold liquid. Solomon and Hiram of Tyre therefore contribute their respective properties of Life-Essence and durable form and " building material " as the groundwork of the soul, which then is made functionally effective by the addition of the third principle described as Hiram Abiff, the widow's son, and personifying the active intellectual principle or Logos. In a word, Hiram Abiff is the Christ-principle immanent in every soul; crucified, dead and buried in all who are not alive to its presence, but resident in all as a saving force—" Christ in you, the hope of glory." Consistently with Christ-like humility, Hiram Abiff (literally, " the teacher from the Father ") is not described as a " king " as are Solomon and Hiram of Tyre, but as one " of no reputation," a " widow's son "; a beautiful touch of Gnostic symbolism referable to the derelict or widowed nature of the Divine Motherhood or Sophia owing to the errancy and defection from wisdom of her frail children. Such of those children as have rejoined, or are striving to rejoin, their mother are alone worthy to be called the " widow's sons," and it is to the cry to those who have rejoined her from those still labouring at that task in the flesh, and perhaps wiping from their brow the bloody sweat of their Gethsemane anguish in the struggle, that the traditional petition applies, " Come to my help, ye sons of the Widow, for I am the Widow's son ! "

The temple of the human soul, primordially constituted of the three principles just spoken of in due balance and proportion and divinely pronounced to be " very good," has deflected from that state. Its fall has been effected by the disproportioned, unbalanced and, therefore, disorderly abuse of its inherent powers. Just as a man in a temper becomes temporarily unbalanced and liable to do what he would not in serene moments, so the soul has disorganized its own nature utterly. Of the three pillars that should support it, Wisdom (Gnosis) has fallen and become replaced by a flexible and shifting prop of speculative opinion : Strength (divine dynamic energy) has become exchanged for the frailty of the perishing flesh : Beauty, the god-like radiant form that should adorn and liken man to his Divine Creator, has become superseded by every ugliness of imperfection. Man is now a ruined temple, over which is written " Ichabod ! Ichabod ! the glory is departed ! " Severed from conscious intercourse with his Vital and Immortal Principle, he is a prisoner in captivity to himself and his lower temporal nature. It remains for him to retrace his steps and rebuild his temple ; to continue no longer a bondslave to his self-made illusions and the attractions of " worldly possessions," but become a free man and mason, engaged in shaping himself into a living and precious stone for the cosmic temple of a regenerate Humanity unto which, when completed and dedicated, Deity will again enter and abide.

To be " installed in the chair of King Solomon," therefore, means in its true sense the reattainment of a Wisdom we have lost and the revival in ourselves of the Divine Life-Essence which is the basis of

our being.   With the reattainment of that Wisdom
all that is comprised in the terms Strength and
Beauty will be reattained also, for the three pillars
stand in eternal association and balance.   Not to
reattain it, not to revive the Divine Life-Essence,
during our sojourn in this world, is to miss the
opportunity which life in physical conditions provides, since the after-death state is one not of
labour at this work, but of refreshment and rest,
where no real progress is possible.   Initiation,
therefore, was instituted to impart the science of
its reattainment and so lift the individual soul to a
new life-basis from which it could proceed to work
out its own salvation and develop its inherent
powers along the true line of its destiny and evolution.   But, as the Ancient Mysteries taught, the
soul that never even begins this work in this world
will not be able to begin it hereafter, but will remain
suspended in the more tenuous planes of this planet
until such time as it is once again indrawn into the
vortex of generation by the ever-turning wheel of
life.   To quote Plato again, " those who instituted
the Mysteries for us taught us that whosoever
descended into Hades (the after-death state)
uninitiated and without being a partaker in the
Mysteries, will be plunged into mire and darkness,
but whoever arrived there purified and initiated will
dwell with the Gods."   This teaching is reproduced
in Masonry in the reference to the Master-Mason
being " admitted to the assembly of the just made
perfect " : the implication being that those who
have not reached that proficiency and are neither
" just " (*i.e.*, rectified) nor perfected, will abide upon

a lower level of post-mortem existence. For the levels of superphysical life are numerous—" in my Father's house are many mansions," or, literally, resting places—and they and their occupants are graduated in hierarchical order according to their degree of fitness and spiritual eminence. The disordered modern world, with its perverse democratic ideals of equality and uniformity, has lost all sense of the hierarchic principle, which since it obtains in the higher world ought to be reflected in this.

> " Order is Heaven's first law and, that confessed,
> Some are, and must be, greater than the rest."

But Masonry preserves the witness to this graduation, and to the existence of separate tiers of life in the heaven-places, in the symbolic distribution of its more advanced members. Above the Craft Lodges there presides the Provincial Grand Lodge ; beyond that rules the Grand Lodge of the nation. Theoretically higher than any of these is the Royal Arch Chapter, with the Provincial and Grand Chapters towering beyond that. In the symbolic clothing worn by the members of each of these ranks the observant student will perceive the intention to give appropriate expression to the truth thereby signified. The Masonic apron has been explained in an earlier paper as a figure of the soul's corporeality—the body (not to be confused with the gross physical body) which it wears and will display when it passes from this life. Its pure white is fringed in the case of junior brethren with a pale shade of that blue which, even in physical nature, is the colour of the heavens. With seniors in the Provincial and Grand Lodges this has intensified to the deepest degree of that hue in correspondence with their theoretical spiritual development, whilst the gold lace adornments of the clothing emblematize what is referred to in the Psalmist's words, " The King's daughter (the soul) is all glorious within; her clothing is of wrought gold " : for as the Life-Essence or Wisdom becomes increasingly " wrought " or substantialized in us, it becomes the objectified corporeality of the soul. In the Royal Arch the Craft devotional blue is intershot with red, the colour of fire or spiritual ardour, the blend resulting in that purple which both in earth and heaven is the prerogative of royalty. Thus, by their clothing in the various grades, the members of Masonry emblematize on earth the angels and archangels and all the company of Heaven. Some of them are clothed with light as with a garment; others are ministers of flaming fire.

In a short paper such as this our reference to the Ancient Mysteries is necessarily brief and has been restricted to the Greek Eleusinian system. Many others of course existed and an extensive, though scattered, literature is available for those who would pursue the subject further in the direction of the Egyptian, Samothracian, Chaldean, Mithraic, Gnostic and other systems. In their respective days and localities they formed the authoritative centres of religion and philosophy, using those terms as but phases of an indivisible subject which nowadays has become split up into many brands of theology and speculative philosophy having little

and often no possible connection with each other.
What the old writers made public about the
Mysteries of course discreetly avoids descriptions
of the deeper truths they imparted or of the actual
processes of initiation. These must always remain
a subject of secrecy, but by the perspicuous reader
enough can be found in their purposely obscure
and metaphorical accounts to indicate what occurred,
and with what effect upon the candidate. Initiation,
we have already said, is something which but few
are fit to receive, even after long and rigorous
preparation, and fewer still are competent to impart.
It was an experience of which a writer has said in
regard to the candidate, *Vel invenit sanctum, vel
facit*—it either finds him holy or makes him so.
Virgil's account in the sixth Æneid of the initiation
of Æneas into Elysium (or the supernatural light),
or that of Lucius (again a name signifying
enlightenment) in the " Golden Ass " of Apuleius,
when he was permitted to " see the sun at midnight,"
are instructive instances. So also the exclamation
of Clement of Alexandria, who had been received
into the Gnostic school : " O truly sacred Mysteries !
O pure Light ! I am led by the light of the torch
to the view of heaven and of God. I become holy
by initiation. The Lord Himself is the hierophant
who, leading the candidate for initiation to the
Light, seals him and presents him to the Father
to be preserved for ever. These are the orgies of
my Mysteries. If thou wilt, come and be thou also
initiated, and thou shalt join in the dance with the
angels around the uncreated, imperishable and only
true God, the Word of God joining in the strain ! "

The Mysteries came to an end as public institutions in the sixth century, when from political considerations they and the teaching of the secret doctrine and philosophy became prohibited by the Roman Government, under Justinian, who aimed at inaugurating an official uniform state-religion throughout its Empire. Subsequently, as the Roman Empire declined and broke up, the Roman Catholic Church emerged from it, which, as we know, has resolutely discountenanced any authority in religion and philosophy as a rival to her own and at the same time claimed supremacy and an over-riding jurisdiction in temporal matters also. For the Freemason the result of that Church's conduct is instructive. For when an authority upon matters wholly spiritual and belonging to a kingdom which is not of this world, lays claim to temporal power and secular possessions, as the Roman Church has done and still does, it at once vitiates and neutralizes its own spiritual qualifications. It becomes infected with the virus of " worldly possessions." It loads itself with the " money and metals " from which it is essential to keep divested. The result has been that what might have been, and was designed to be, the greatest spiritually educative force in the world's history, has become a materialized institution, exercising an intellectual tyranny which has estranged the minds of millions from religion altogether. As Lot's wife is metaphorically said to have crystallized into a pillar of salt through turning back in desire to what she ought to have renounced altogether, so in trying to serve Mammon and God at the same time the Roman Church has failed in both and, as the result of the false steps and abuses of centuries. the world is to-day a chaos of disunited sects and popular religious teaching is as materialistic as Masonry. It is a pity, for in its original design and practice Christianity was intended to serve as a system of initiation upon a catholic or universal scale, and to take over, supersede and amplify all that previously was taught, in a less efficacious way and to a more restricted public, in the Ancient Mysteries. It is not possible here to enter upon the extremely interesting questions involved in the transition from pre-Christian to Christian religion, or to explain why and how the Christian Mysteries are the efflorescence of the earlier ones and transcend them. In their central teachings, as in the philosophic method of life they demand, the two methods are identical. The differences between them are only such as are due to amplification and formal expression. Christianity came not to destroy, but to fulfil and expand. That fulfilment and expansion were consequent upon an event of cosmic importance which we speak of as The Incarnation. By that event something had happened affecting the very fabric of our planet and every item of the human family. What that something was and the nature of the change it wrought is too great and deep a theme to develop now, but, to illustrate it by Masonic symbolism, it was an event which is the equivalent of, and is represented by, the transference of the Sacred Symbol of the Grand Geometrician of the Universe from the ceiling of the Lodge, where it is located in the elementary grades of the Craft, to the floor, where it is found in the Royal

Arch Degree surrounded with flaming lights and every circumstance of reverence and sanctity. How many Masons are there in the Order to-day who recognize that, in this piece of symbolism, Masonry is giving affirmation and ocular testimony to precisely the same fact as the churchman affirms when he recites in his Creed the words " He came down from heaven, and was incarnate and was made man ? "

By a tacit and quite unwarranted convention the members of the Craft avoid mention in their Lodges of the Christian Master and confine their scriptural readings and references almost exclusively to the Old Testament, the motive being no doubt due to a desire to observe the injunction as to refraining from religious discussion and to prevent offence on the part of brethren who may not be of the Christian faith. The motive is an entirely misguided one and is negated by the fact that the " greater light " upon which every member is obligated, and to which his earnest attention is recommended from the moment of his admission to the Order, is not only the Old Testament, but the volume of the Sacred Law in its entirety. The New Testament is as essential to his instruction as the Old, not merely because of its moral teaching, but in virtue of its constituting the record of the Mysteries in their supreme form and historic culmination. The Gospels themselves, like the Masonic degrees, are a record of preparation and illumination, leading up to the ordeal of death, followed by a raising from the dead and the attainment of Mastership, and they exhibit the process of initiation carried to the highest conceivable degree of attainment. The New Testament is full of passages in Masonic terminology and there is not a little irony in the failure by modern Masons to recognize its supreme importance and relevancy to their Lodge proceedings and in the fact that in so doing they may be likening themselves to those builders of whom it is written that they rejected the chief Corner Stone. They would learn further that the Grand Master and Exemplar of Masonry, Hiram Abiff, is but a figure of the Great Master and Exemplar and Saviour of the world, the Divine Architect by whom all things were made, without whom is nothing that hath been made, and whose life is the light of men. If, in the words of the Masonic hymn :

> " Hiram the architect
> Did all the Craft direct
> How they should build,"

it is equally true that the protagonist of the Christian Scriptures also taught universal humanity " how they should build " and reconstruct their own fallen nature, and that the method of such building is one which involves the cross as its working tool and one which culminates in a death and a raising from the dead. And, of those who attain their initiation and mastership by that method, is it not further written there that they become of the household of God and built into a spiritual temple not made with hands, but eternal and in the heavens and of which "Jesus Christ is the chief corner stone, in whom all the building, fitly framed together, groweth unto an holy temple builded for an habitation of God ?"

Neither the Ancient Mysteries nor Modern Masonry, their descendant, therefore, can be rightly viewed without reference to their relation to the Christian evangel, into which the pre-Christian schools became assumed. The line of succession and evolution from the former to the latter is direct and organic. Allowing for differences of time, place and form of expression, both taught exactly the same truths and inculcated the necessity for regeneration. In such a matter there cannot be a diversity of doctrine. The truth concerning it must be static and uniform at all periods of the world's history. Hence we find St. Augustine affirming that there has never existed but one religion in the world since the beginning of time (meaning by religion the science of rebinding the dislocated soul to its source), and that that religion began to be called Christian in apostolic times. And hence too it is that both the Roman Church and Masonry, although so widely divergent in outlook and method, have this feature in common, that each declares and insists that no alteration or innovation in its central doctrine is permissible and that it is unlawful to remove or deviate from its ancient landmarks. Each is right in its insistence, for in the system of each is enshrined the age-old doctrine of regeneration and divinization of the human soul, obscured in the one case by theological and other accretions foreign to the main purpose of religion, and unperceived in the other because its symbolism remains uninterpreted. To clear vision, Christian and Masonic doctrine are identical in intention though different in method. The one says " *Via*

Crucis "; the other " *Via Lucis* "; yet the two ways are but one way. The former teaches through the ear; the latter through the eye and by identifying the aspirant with the doctrine by passing him personally and dramatically through symbolic rites which he is expected to translate from ceremonial form into subjective experience. As Patristic literature shows, the primitive method of the Christian Church was not that which now obtains, under which the religious offices and teaching are administered to the whole public alike and in a way implying a common level of doctrine for all and uniform power of comprehension by every member of the congregation. It was, on the other hand, a graduated method of instruction and identical with the Masonic system of degrees conferred by reason of advancing merit and ability. To cite one of the most instructive of early Christian treatises (Dionysius : *On the Ecclesiastical Hierarchy*), with which every Masonic student should familiarize himself, it will be found that admission to the early Church was by three ceremonial degrees exactly corresponding in intention with those of Masonry. " The most holy initiation of the Mystic Rites has as its first Godly purpose the holy cleansing of the initiated ; and as second, the enlightening instruction of the purified ; and finally and as the completion of the former, the perfecting of those instructed in the science of their appropriate instructions. The order of the Ministers in the first class cleanses the initiated through the Mystic Rites ; in the second, conducts the purified to light ; and, in the last and highest, makes perfect those who have participated in the Divine Light by the

scientific contemplations of the illuminations contemplated." This brief passage alone suffices to
show that originally membership of the Christian
Church involved a sequence of three initiatory rites
identical in intention with those of the Craft to-day.
The names given to those who had qualified in
those Rites were respectively Catechumens,
Leiturgoi, and Priests or Presbyters; which in
turn are identifiable with our Entered Apprentices,
Fellow Crafts and Master Masons. Their first
degree was that of a rebirth and purification of the
heart; their second related to the illumination of
the intelligence; and their third to a total death
unto sin and a new birth unto righteousness, in
which the candidate died with Christ on the cross,
as with us he is made to imitate the death of Hiram,
and was raised to that higher order of life which is
Mastership.

When Christianity became a state-religion and the
Church a world-power, the materialization of its
doctrine proceeded apace and has only increased
with the centuries. Instead of becoming the
unifying force its leaders meant it to be, its association with " worldly possessions " has resulted in
making it a disintegrative one. Abuses led to
schisms and sectarianism, and whilst the parent-
body, in the form of the Greek and Roman Churches,
still possesses and jealously conserves all the original
credentials, traditions and symbols in their superb
liturgies and rites, more importance is attached to the
outer husk of its heritage than to its kernel and spirit,
whilst the Protestant communities and so-called
"free" churches have unhappily become self-severed

*Free-
masonry
in
Relation
to the
Ancient
Mysteries*

211

altogether from the original tradition and their imagined liberty and independence are in fact but a captivity to ideas of their own, having no relation to the primitive gnosis and no understanding of those Mysteries which must always lie deeper than the exoteric popular religion of a given period. Regeneration as a science has long been, and still is, entirely outside the purview of orthodox religion. The Christian Master's affirmation " Ye must be born again " is regarded as but a pious counsel towards an indefinite improvement of conduct and character, not as a reference to a drastic scientific revolution and reformation of the individual in the way contemplated by the rites of initiation prescribed in the Mysteries. Popular religion may indeed produce " good " men, as the world's standard of goodness goes. It does not and cannot produce divinized men endued with the qualities of Mastership, for it is ignorant of the traditional wisdom and methods by which that end is to be attained.

That wisdom and those traditional methods of the Mysteries have, however, never been without living witness in the world, despite the jealousy and inhibitions of official orthodoxy. Since the suppression of the Mysteries in the sixth century, their tradition and teaching have been continued in secret and under various concealments, and to that continuation our present Masonic system is due. As previously intimated in these papers, it was compiled and projected between two and three centuries ago as an elementary expression of the ancient doctrine and initiatory method, by a group of minds which were far more deeply instructed in the old tradition

and secret science than are those who avail themselves of their work to-day, or even than the text
of the Masonic rites indicates. If they remained
obscure and anonymous, so that the modern
student's research is unable to identify them, it is
only what is to be expected, for the true initiate is
one who never proclaims himself as such and is
content ever to remain impersonal and out of sight
and notoriety, planting his seed for the welfare of
his fellow men indifferently and leaving others to
water it and God to give it increase. But, within
the limits they allowed themselves, they achieved
their work well and truly and, as has been sought
to demonstrate in these pages, made it a rescript,
faithful at least in outline and main principles, of
the ancient teaching and perfecting rites of the
philosophic Mysteries. It has been well said by a
writer of authority on the subject that they put
forward the system of speculative Masonry as " an
experiment upon the mind of the age," and with a
view to exhibiting to at least a small section of a
public living in a time of gross darkness and
materialism an evidence of the doctrine of
regeneration which might serve as a light to such
as could profit therefrom. If this theory be true,
their intention may at first sight appear to have
become falsified by subsequent developments, in
the course of which there has sprung up an organization of world-wide dimensions and vast membership,
animated undoubtedly in the main with worthy
ideals and accomplishing a certain measure of
benevolent work, but nevertheless failing entirely
in perceiving its true and original purpose as an

*Free-
masonry
in
Relation
to the
Ancient
Mysteries*

213

Order for promoting the science of human regeneration, and unconscious that by this default its achieve-
ments in other directions are of small or no account.
But a broader and wiser view of the situation would
be one that, whilst recognizing a great diffusion
of energy to little present purpose, sees also that,
in the long run and in the amplitude of time, that
energy is not wasted but conserved, and that, besides
benefiting individuals here and there who are capable
of truly profiting from the Order, it preserves the
witness and keeps burning the light of the perpetual
Mysteries in a dark age. Like the light of a Master
Mason which never becomes wholly extinguished,
so in the world's darkest days the light of the
Mysteries never goes out entirely, and God and the
way to Him are not left without witness. If, in
comparison with other witnesses, Masonry is but a
glimmering ray rather than a powerful beam of
light, it is none the less a true ray; a kindly light lit
from the world's central altar-flame, and sufficing to
lead at least some of us on amid the encircling gloom,
until the night is gone. Light is granted in proportion to the desire of our hearts, but for the majority
of Masons their Order sheds no light at all, because
light is not their desire, nor is initiation in its true
sense understood or wished for. They move among
the symbols, simulacra and substituted secrets of the
Mysteries without comprehending them, without
wishing to translate them into reality. The Craft is
made to subserve social and philanthropic ends
foreign to its purpose and even to gratify the desire
for outward personal distinction; but as an instrument of regeneration it remains wholly ineffective.

214

Is this nescience, this imperviousness and failure to comprehend, however, to no purpose? Perhaps not. Each of us lives in the presence of natural mysteries he fails to discern or understand, and even when the desire for wisdom is at last awakened, the education of the understanding is a long process. Nature in all her kingdoms builds slowly, perfecting her aims through endless repetitions and apparently wanton waste of material. And in the things of the Kingdom which transcends Nature, the same method prevails. Souls are drawn but slowly to the Light, and their perfecting and transmutation into that Light is often very gradual. For long before it is able to distinguish shadow from substance, Humanity must try its prentice-hand upon illusory toys and substitutions for the genuine secrets of Reality. For long before it is worthy of actual initiation upon the path that leads to God it must be permitted to indulge in preliminary unintelligent rehearsals of the processes therein involved. The approaches to the ancient temples of the Mysteries were lined with statues of the Gods, having no value of themselves, but intended to habituate the minds of neophytes to the spiritual concepts and divine attributes to which those statues were meant to give objective form and semblance. But within the temple itself all graven images, all formal figures, symbols and ceremonial types, ceased; for the mind had then finally to learn to dispense with their help, and, in the strength of its own purity and understanding alone, to rise into unclouded perception of their formless prototypes and " see the Nameless of the hundred names."

Free-masonry in Relation to the Ancient Mysteries

215

" Get knowledge, get wisdom ; but with all thy gettings, get understanding," exclaims the old Teacher, in a counsel that may well be commended to the Masonic Fraternity to-day, which so little understands its own system. But understanding depends upon the gift of the Supernal Light, which gift in turn depends upon the ardour of our desire for it. If Wisdom to-day is widowed, all Masons are actually or potentially the widow's sons, and she will be justified of her children who seek her out and who labour for her as for hid treasure. It remains with the Craft itself whether it shall enter upon its own heritage as a lineal successor of the Ancient Mysteries and Wisdom-teaching, or whether, by failing so to do, it will undergo the inevitable fate of everything that is but a form from which its native spirit has departed.